FACILITATING
ONLINE LEARNING
Effective Strategies for Moderators

Atwood
Publishing
Madison, WI

GEORGE COLLISON

BONNIE ELBAUM

SARAH HAAVIND

ROBERT TINKER

Facilitating Online Learning:
Effective Stratgies for Moderators
by George Collison, Bonnie Elbaum, Sarah Haavind, Robert Tinker

© 2000
Atwood Publishing
2710 Atwood Ave.
Madison, WI 53704
888.242.7101
www.atwoodpublishing.com

Printed in the United States of America

Cover and text design © TLC Graphics, www.TLCGraphics.com

Library of Congress Cataloging-in-Publication Data

Facilitating online learning: effective strategies for moderators / by
George Collison ... [et al.].
    p. cm.
Includes bibliographical references.
  ISBN 1-891859-33-1 (pbk.)
  1. Computer conferencing in education. 2. Teaching--Computer network
resources. 3. Instructional systems--Design. 4. Group facilitation.
I. Collison, George, 1946-
  LB1044.875 .F33 2000
  371.33'4--dc21
                        00-010672

This work was supported by a grant by the National Science Foundation.

TABLE OF CONTENTS

11451

ABOUT THE AUTHORS
AND ACKNOWLEDGMENTS

■ ■ ■ ■ ■ ■ ■ ■ ■ ■

▶

████████ The primary authors of this book are all members of the staff of The Concord Consortium, a nonprofit research and development organization in Concord, Massachusetts. The Consortium is dedicated to revolutionizing education through the use of information technologies:

George Collison, PhD is the academic director of the INTEC (International Netcourse Teacher Enhancement Coalition) Project, a suite of professional development netcourses that support teachers who are bringing inquiry-based approaches into their mathematics or science classrooms. George first articulated the vision for INTEC, and he trained INTEC moderators to implement our successful approach to facilitating online learning communities.

Bonnie Elbaum works with the Virtual High School (VHS), a collaborative of high schools from around the United States that, in exchange for contributing a small amount of teaching time, can offer their students a choice of 200+ netcourses — ranging from advanced academic courses to technical and specialized courses — to augment local curriculum offerings.

Sarah Haavind designs and teaches online courses for the Consortium, including the INTEC netcourses and a sequence of courses that support learning the moderating techniques presented in this book.

Robert Tinker, PhD is internationally recognized as a pioneer in constructivist uses of educational technologies. He developed the idea of using probes, such as the ultrasonic motion detector, for student learning based on real-time measurements. He also was the first person to use electronic networking to permit students to collaborate on dispersed environment investigations. The initial result of this work was the NGS Kids Network, the first curriculum making extensive use of student collaboration and data sharing. This early success led to the Global Lab and GLOBE projects as well as the development of LabNet, an early use of networking to support teachers' professional development. Six years ago, Robert founded The Concord Consortium. His current research includes work on the educational applications of portable computers, large-scale tests of online courses for teachers and secondary students, sophisticated simulations, and the development of technology-rich materials for sustainable development education.

You'll find that this book is also filled with excerpts from online discussions, presented anonymously. Our virtual colleagues — both participants in and facilitators from our netcourses — have graciously granted us permission to use their crafted postings as examples throughout the book. They are: Peter Atlas, Nancy Borchers, Lisa Bulthuis, Russell Burck, Peggy Collins, Ed Eckel, Sherry Hsi, Matt Huston, Sarah Inkpen, Susan Leavey, Tom Long, Pat Martin, Julia Maxey, Vicki McMillian, Francis Morse, Michelle Murrain, Sigrin T. Newell, Andrew Njaa, Bill Peruzzi, Carol Philips, Sandra Grace Pyeatt, Kathy Renfrew, David Senecal, Alan Shapiro, Yvonne Sims, Luron Singer, Don Smith, Wanda Stuckley, Edgar Taylor, Helen M. Trencher, and Marsha West. Nick Noakes and others who have taken our course on moderating, based on a draft of this book, have helped us clarify our thinking about the strategies contained herein, and for that assistance as well we are most grateful.

Special thanks go to master critical thinker Judith Collison of The Concord Consortium for her edits and insights in framing the chapters on critical thinking strategies and the roadblocks to dialogue. We are grateful to Cynthia McIntyre, the INTEC project coordinator, for her tireless editing of early drafts and contribution of the section on Virtual "Hand Holding" (Chapter 3). Additional contributions have been made by members of Consortium staff, Raymond Rose, Barbara Tinker, Lee McDavid, Jeannie Finks, and David Pitkin.

Our special thanks also go to Publisher Linda Babler of Atwood Publishing, for believing in us and supporting this work; our kind and gentle editor, Peter Vogt, for his careful reading and insightful suggestions; and Tamara Dever and Erin Stark of TLC Graphics, our book designers. This has truly been a collaboration to meet a brand new need: deepening online learning. And since we have nurtured social knowledge construction in the online discussion spaces for our netcourses, it follows that this book of e-learning has evolved as a project of collaborative knowledge building, with many supporting builders along the way. Our thanks to all.

INTRODUCTION

Netcourse *(NET-kors)*: n. A body of study offered via world-wide digital electronic communications; derived from the term network, referring to a system of associated computers that facilitates the sharing of information.

Moderator *(ma-de-RA-ter)*: n. A person charged with fostering the culture and the learning in an online dialogue or in a net-course discussion area.

A participant (herself a teacher) in an online professional development course, or netcourse, completes a science activity with fellow teachers in her local, face-to-face study group. She then makes this comment in the course's interactive discussion area:

> The experiment was fun to do and a learning experience for me. At first, the experiment appeared to be useless in the sense that the marbles did as expected. The value of the activity was not in the weighing or dropping of the marbles, or in any other part of the experiment. For me, the *value of the experiment was in the online discussion that followed.*

That discussion was facilitated by a highly skilled *moderator.*

WHAT IS THIS BOOK ABOUT?

Effective moderation is a critical but often forgotten aspect of turning a net-course or online discussion group into a goal-oriented learning community.

As more businesses and schools connect to the Internet, and access to new technologies increases, the use of online communication for teaching and training nationwide and worldwide will continue to grow. It's certainly already true that high-quality netcourses can point participants to the latest best practices in any field. Now, it is becoming increasingly true that instructors can more easily access the support of experts and colleagues online as they work to enhance learning in their virtual classrooms. Likewise, the assistance of talented web masters and media design staff brings increasingly appealing and user-friendly layouts to the presentation of any quality netcourse.

But beyond the availability of engaging presentations and quality content, there is another yardstick against which any netcourse must be measured: the *skill of the facilitator*. Can he or she lead virtual community participants to focus and deepen their growth and learning via online dialogue? Course design and presentation mechanisms, together with excellence in online dialogue facilitation, separate the excellent online course from the mediocre or weak one.

As interest in taking and offering online courses grows, so too does the technology that makes it possible. However, the new, powerful advantages of *asynchronous* learning environments in an information-infused global society are unlikely to fade with better, faster, and *smoother* synchronous technologies. And increasingly, professionals are changing the meaning of the work day and work week by telecommuting. We, as a society, are also making more time for family, friendships, and personal hobbies.

The netcourses we offer and engage in must meet these new demands. The challenges of synchronous scheduling, especially internationally, will not be the only deterrent as more people discover the inherent advantages of the asynchronous netcourse and virtual conference room. Guiding moderators in the techniques and skills they need to facilitate professional online dialogue is an important next step in effectively using the wealth of online opportunities available for the personal and professional growth of people around the world.

A NEW WORLD OF TEACHING AND LEARNING

Early on in the Virtual High School (a network of high schools around the U.S. that offer their students a choice of 200+ netcourses, ranging from advanced academic courses to technical and specialized courses), we detected a degree of trust and safety among the involved teachers that ignited a level of collaboration we'd never before encountered. For instance, during the first months of the collaboration, when teachers were building their netcourses, a teacher in California asked for other teachers in training to "visit" her new netcourse and check it out. "Is it interesting? Does it flow? Do the links work? Does the content make sense?," were her questions. Within a week, several teachers from around the country had given her the requested feedback — *and* they had asked that their own courses be similarly scrutinized. Before long, all thirty teachers in the group were receiving feedback from their peers in twenty-two other states.

We asked the teachers if they'd previously exhibited a natural tendency to walk down the hall in their brick-and-mortar schools to have peers review their lesson plans. Not one had ever done that. "Well, then, why are you doing it online?" one of us asked. The reply came from another California teacher. "Because I can't hear anybody laughing at me here."

Moderated discussions have become a standard component of the world of digital communication, including netcourses. Many educators have lauded the added value of asynchronous, text-based discussion. Numerous manuals have been published, online and off, about appropriate 'netiquette (Internet etiquette) and successful strategies for facilitating constructive online discussion. Many of the associated suggestions are based on analogues or transference of techniques that have been developed and polished in face-to-face dialogue.

Online discussion is in some ways quite similar to face-to-face meetings. Yet, in other ways, it is subtly and profoundly different. In our work with online courses at The Concord Consortium, we've found that beyond classroom teaching skills brought to the online forums, there are specific strategies and a wide palette of voices and tones that a professor, teacher, trainer, or online moderator can use to focus and move a discussion forward. Knowledgeable use of such strategies can enrich and deepen the dialogue and foster learning in this emerging venue.

That's where *Facilitating Online Learning: Effective Strategies for Moderators* comes in.

WHY THIS BOOK?

The number of virtual learning communities is bound to increase greatly in years to come. As netcourses reach new widely scattered and specialized audiences, more people will join in, both as facilitators and as participants. It is critical, then, that those leading such goal-driven environments be as skilled as possible in fostering rich online dialogue. Otherwise, the potential of even the highest-quality online courses goes to waste.

Many of the facilitation skills for the online venue, described in this book, are also perfectly suited for face-to-face dialogue, particularly for a quick-witted discussion leader who is sensitive to nuance, content, and social context. Such skills are difficult to master and apply in a live interaction; this is, perhaps, the reason why an excellent meeting facilitator is so highly valued in any workplace. On the other hand, online learning communities may be accessible to a wider spectrum of potential leaders: Many capable people who lack natural charisma in a live context are presented with a different opportunity online.

Case in point: When asked to present at a professional conference, one very talented online moderator responded:

> Oh, no. I don't present myself well. I'm not that attractive and my voice is too mousy.

While we're a long way from developing a profile of characteristics or attributes possessed by skilled online moderators, humility, the capacity to listen (read!) carefully, and the ability to respond without interjecting personal or professional opinions or values seem to be characteristics shared by the most successful practitioners. Needless to say, this is not the usual list of top criteria for successful group leadership in face-to-face settings! In fact, this new, digital venue calls for a reconsideration of many of the standard discussion-leading techniques. Two simple examples — *wait time* (stopping for more than a few seconds after posing a question to a group) and *redirection* (pulling elements from what has been said to refocus a potentially tangential discussion back on to learning objectives) — illustrate some fundamental differences between face-to-face and online discussions/presentations.

Wait time, so important in face-to-face meetings, takes on a completely new meaning online. Online wait time — a period of sustained reflection about a participant's or facilitator's posting — can be measured in hours or even days, not seconds around a conference table. This fosters opportunities for rich thinking and response that are unheard of in a live setting.

Redirection, a standard technique for workshop or discussion leaders, relies on capturing salient points while they are still fresh in the memories of the audience and using only those points to guide the group in a direction the facilitator deems productive. Online text forums, with sequenced written records, provide ready evidence for alternative interpretation or refocusing. Skilled moderators recognize the potential of the traditional redirection technique and can incorporate it with ease at their leisure. Even connections that would be far too subtle to make in a real-time, aural-based setting can be explored and deepened more simply when the record is permanent text.

Online moderators also report that they more fully develop in their capacity to lead dialogue in the "regular" brick-and-mortar setting. One of our netcourse participants noted:

> [Since my netcourse experiences,] I've been altering my teaching methods within my four-walled classroom to reflect the discussion/group-type activities we've been using [online].

WHO WILL BENEFIT FROM READING THIS BOOK?

You're a teacher faced with putting a course online — and you have no idea how to go about it. Or maybe you're already teaching an online course or moderating an online discussion group — and you're feeling overwhelmed. Or perhaps you're being deluged with private emails from your online course participants, not to mention reams of public postings that you must review, recap, or grade — all in addition to designing assignments for the online environment.

If any of these or similar scenarios sound familiar to you, you're not alone.

Would you rather spend your online time improving your ability to create forward momentum in your discussion or course, focusing the direction of the participants' dialogue, and deepening discussions so that the most pertinent issues are addressed? Then this book is definitely for you!

College professors, corporate managers and trainers, secondary school teachers, and others will find in these pages strategies to enrich their skill at online facilitation and discussion moderation.

WHAT WILL YOU LEARN FROM THIS BOOK?

In Chapter 1, "Principles that Support Effective Moderating," we identify three fundamental principles that have emerged from our project work.

They may seem rather obvious on the surface, but in fact, acknowledging these realities in your course or project design and style of leadership can be the difference between effective and useless moderation. The principles:

- Moderating takes place in both a professional and a social context.
- The style of "Guide on the Side" (vs. "Sage on the Stage") is most appropriate for leading a virtual learning community.
- Online moderation is a craft that has general principles and strategies — which you can learn.

Chapter 2, "Negotiating Space: Forms of Dialogue and Goals of Moderating," sets the stage for creating a culture of learning in your netcourse or virtual teamwork. There are patterns of speaking that we call *forms of dialogue* you must recognize and channel if you want to enhance learning in the virtual classroom. The predominant forms of dialogue commonly evident in online discussions:

- Social dialogue
- Argumentative dialogue
- Pragmatic dialogue

If you're an experienced online moderator, you've seen how social dialogue or argumentative dialogue can close down discussions that otherwise would have helped to meet the goals and objectives of the course or online teamwork you're leading. Fostering pragmatic dialogue, alternatively, helps maintain a productive focus and move a virtual community toward its goals.

In Chapter 3, "Key Facilitator Roles," we look at three key roles you'll play as a moderator: "Guide on the Side," instructor or project leader, and group process facilitator. Among other things, we examine how your role can shift depending on circumstances and your students.

In Chapter 4, "Healthy Online Communities," we offer a "manual within a book" of basic strategies for maintaining functional online groups. If you're already a practiced moderator, you might want to simply scan this chapter and move directly to the advanced strategies that follow.

Chapters 5, 6, and 7 offer you a "tool kit" or palette of advanced strategies that will ensure pragmatic dialogue in your virtual discussion areas. Chapter 5 examines "Voice." Voices offer diagnoses of what a discussion might need to move forward. Chapter 6, "Tone," examines how you can offer empathy to participants and nurture people who are struggling with new content or new design challenges. And in Chapter 7, we offer some proven "Critical Thinking Strategies" you might use to focus or deepen an ongoing discussion at critical junctures.

Finally, in Chapter 8 — "Roadblocks and Getting Back on Track" — we discuss a number of classic roadblocks you're likely to face (if you're like the rest of us when we moderate!). You need to watch out for these roadblocks, which even the best of moderators can inadvertently put up in discussions — despite interjecting with the best of intentions.

THE BACKDROP FOR THIS BOOK

The framework for our research and our development of the vision and capacity to support online teaching and learning is The Concord Consortium Educational Technology Lab. The Concord Consortium was founded in 1994 in Concord, Massachusetts. Headed by Robert Tinker, the Consortium's central goal is to implement the educational promise of technology. Effective facilitation of netcourses is an essential aspect of our work.

Two projects conceived and administered by the Consortium — the Virtual High School® Cooperative (VHS) and the International Netcourse Teacher Enhancement Coalition (INTEC) — provide the setting and structure for the work described in this book.

VHS (see the web site vhs.concord.org) is a $7.4 million project funded by a 1996 Technology Innovation Challenge Grant from the U.S. Department of Education. (Learn more about these grants at the web site www.ed.gov.) VHS provides online courses to over five thousand students across the United States and around the world. We train VHS teachers to design and present courses in an online format, in a course we call the Teacher Learning Conference — or, more affectionately, the TLC. Participants learn how to use Lotus database software called LearningSpace (see the web site www.lotus.com/home.nsf/tabs/learnspace). They then must have a course ready to offer for the opening of the next academic year in the Virtual High School. Their challenges and motivations do not differ much from those found in corporate training contexts, where producing a high-quality product or following an exact process is crucial.

INTEC (see the web site www.intec.concord.org) — funded by a $3 million, four-year National Science Foundation (NSF) grant — began in 1996. It's a course for middle-school and secondary math and science teachers who want to improve their practices by incorporating inquiry-based pedagogy and curriculum materials into their classrooms. As professional development offered for graduate credit, it is similar to many academic course offerings in that moving to more inquiry-based teaching practices is largely a conceptual learning goal.

In both of these efforts, our challenge at the Consortium is to create effective strategies for scaling such courses so that they might be offered to hundreds, or even thousands, of teachers. The ease of access to the Internet challenges us to maximize the scalability of high-quality academic and training courses. We have shown that school districts and schools can realize significant cost savings by offering professional development delivered via netcourses. Why? Because there are no substitute teachers, transportation, or room-and-board expenses for either the participants themselves or their "cyber faculty." The cost for high-quality instruction is much lower than in traditional approaches, and its accessibility is greater as well. It's possible to scale teacher professional development netcourses to reach national audiences, and at one-half the cost of today's summer institutes.

The key to realizing this economy of scale lies in the capacity to shift the responsibility of performing the moderating function away from the original course or content developers and to any number of trained facilitators. We've discovered that it is possible to, in a reasonable amount of time, train moderators to support the learning or improvement goals of a netcourse that's been designed by others (e.g., an expert team within a given field or combination of fields). A pyramid structure of expert moderators, trained moderators, and moderators-in-training brings to reality — without sacrificing quality — the concept of offering an excellent netcourse anytime, anywhere to anyone who's interested.

This book serves those who have never tried facilitating online dialogue and who seek to gather information about the process from experienced practitioners. It also serves seasoned online course facilitators who wish to confirm their own understandings of moderation, reflect on their own practices, and, perhaps, expand their repertoire of strategies for effective online training or teaching.

However you approach the book, we hope you'll find it useful — and we welcome your feedback on it. To contact the authors or join a discussion of the book, visit the website: www.concord.org/books/fol

Chapter One

PRINCIPLES THAT SUPPORT EFFECTIVE MODERATING

If you're moderating an online discussion forum, it's probably for either a netcourse or a goal-oriented project group — or something roughly analogous to either or both. It's probably also the case that a face-to-face version of the same course exists, the reason for it being originally determined by corporate or institutional needs.

But it is assuredly not the case that the shift from a traditional course to a web offering of the same content is an easy one. HTML aside, there are larger issues with which to contend when transitioning from course models derived from a face-to-face setting. How do participants engage with ideas, experiment with their application, and communicate with the instructor and their colleagues or classmates, who are also part of the learning community? And how are educational objectives met in a virtual context?

The quick answer: Through the use of text-based, moderated discussion areas. Participants need to interact with each other and the facilitator to share insights and explore ideas.

An online "interaction," however, takes on a different shape than its face-to-face counterpart. A talented lecturer or workshop leader is finely attuned to the nuances of his or her audience. But in the virtual world, there is no body language from which the instructor can gauge the interest of the participants and, consequently, adjust the tone or pace of the presentation. So accommodations in voice, style, and expectations must be made to support virtual facilitation.

Online discussion areas offer many advantages you won't find in face-to-face settings. Text-based, *asynchronous* (not in real time) dialogue can, for instance, greatly extend reflection time; many facilitators and participants welcome the opportunity to compose thoughtful, probing contributions. Furthermore, virtual discussions provide little place for "disengaged" participants to hide or to fake their involvement; silence or non-substantive comments in text form reveal nonparticipation that is more likely to be overlooked in a face-to-face setting, where silence could simply mean that others filled limited airtime, not that the quiet ones weren't engaged. Finally, participants can access vast resources through hyperlinks for comparison or research within a dialogue.

With these benefits in mind, we believe the question before the next generation of course designers and facilitators is: How can the advantages afforded by the cyber venue be optimally used to improve upon even *real*-time and *real*-place educational sessions?

As more corporate and educational institutions move online in search of quality instruction or training, it's essential that professors, teachers, and other course designers, as well as the facilitators who will actually lead virtual communities, consider several alternative methods and tools available for effective online moderating. This book offers a foundation for supporting a new cadre of online facilitators and expanding their repertoire of strategies to support virtual learning. Those that excel in this role may not be the same people who currently provide models of excellence in face-to-face workshop training or physical classroom forms of instruction. Happily, given a useful road map, successful moderating is much easier in the text environment, where new strategies need not be ready on the fly, moment to moment, as is the case when one is facilitating real-time dialogue.

Online professional dialogue relies on sophisticated telecommunications and technologies. While the complexity and capacity in these fields certainly will increase over time, our approach to online moderating is based on a pedagogical foundation of *guided inquiry*, not on particular technologies. Educational reform efforts sponsored by the National Science Foundation place learning through inquiry-based pedagogy front and center. In the field of training in business and industry, inquiry, as a conceptual and pedagogical tool, occupies an important place in the work of such renowned experts as Peter Senge and Chris Argyris.

For netcourse or project team participants, inquiry in dialogue emerges from a course design that enables them to *construct their own knowledge, together.* The facilitated online discussion is the container for this construction of meaning and useful outcomes. The idea of designing instruction and dialogue to facilitate the personal building of knowledge is certainly not new. Some argue that this method was employed by practitioners from fourth century B.C. Athens, by Renaissance educators like Vico, and, in our time, by followers of John Dewey and case study and management experts in law and business. The challenge we address in this book centers on how technology can successfully mediate and enhance this powerful technique, in text-based, asynchronous environments.

Here at The Concord Consortium, in the context of two major netcourses we created and have now offered for the past five years, we've developed a set of principles for the cyber classroom that support effective learning in online dialogues. Below, we describe these two courses as well as the moderating principles that have proven effective for leading and facilitating netcourses.

CONSORTIUM NETCOURSES

Throughout this book, we draw upon actual examples from two Concord Consortium netcourses that already have been offered to thousands of participants. We present brief descriptions of these netcourses here to provide a context for the repertoire of moderating strategies we've found most beneficial for virtual growth and learning.

International Netcourse Teacher Enhancement Coalition (INTEC)

The International Netcourse Teacher Enhancement Coalition (INTEC) provides secondary mathematics and science teachers with a graduate-level professional development course that increases their knowledge of inquiry-based instruction. INTEC is designed to be an alternative to the summer residential professional development institutes that the National Science Foundation has funded for many years. Aside from a general introduction to the pedagogy of inquiry-based instruction, the course introduces participants to eleven exemplary curricula. Each teacher selects one curriculum for in-depth study. He or she then designs and pilots a two- to four-week, inquiry-based unit in his or her own classroom.

INTEC's approach to professional development is based on an innovative hybrid model for a netcourse that combines face-to-face activities with individual and online activities. Participants join the project by signing up as local study groups (LSGs) of four or more, usually situated at the same school.

Designed by experts in content and pedagogy, the INTEC netcourse provides online reading material and activities for all participants. They meet virtually with an online Field Expert and other participants who have chosen the same curriculum to study. The Field Experts are teachers who have already used the materials in their classrooms. Participants also meet regularly at LSG meetings to discuss their ideas.

Though the Internet is a critical component of INTEC, it is not used exclusively. Books, software, videos, and other materials that support the course are regularly shipped to participants.

INTEC's instructional designers don't interact directly with participants in this model. Moderators and Field Experts guide groups of twenty to forty participants through the course topics. INTEC staff coach the moderators, help them solve problems, troubleshoot any software or design issues they run into, and coach them on how to act as "Guides on the Side" for their participants.

Teacher Learning Conference (TLC)

The Teacher Learning Conference (TLC) is a training course offered by The Concord Consortium to groups seeking to create collaborative netcourses in LearningSpace, a distance-learning platform or courseware. The TLC primarily serves teachers who are participating in the Virtual High School (VHS) collaborative of accredited high schools whose teachers lead a virtual course in exchange for seats for local students in the VHS. The collaborative now offers over two hundred teacher-designed netcourses for high school students.

The charge of teachers in the TLC is to craft an Internet-based academic course as they move through the twenty-five weeks of TLC training. Schools participating in the VHS collaborative gain a range of courses to add to their offerings, at low cost and without expanding local enrollment or staff. In exchange for providing a teacher and a course taught by that teacher in the VHS course catalog, each school in the VHS cooperative can enroll twenty students in any other VHS netcourse being offered by other participating schools.

The goal of the TLC is not simply to give instructors technological and other skills. TLC participants also experience interactions with course moderators and share in the moderating, thus practicing the type of facilitation and support they're expected to include in their own courses. By the end of the course, each VHS teacher will have created his or her own unique netcourse, and will also be ready to deliver it effectively to twenty high school students nationwide via the Internet.

Central to both INTEC and the TLC is the use of *scheduled, asynchronous assignments*. This design combines the advantages of self-paced study (flexibility with regard to when to work on assignments) with the benefits of synchronous courses, in which all participants attend class at the same moment. The courses require weekly assignments to be completed at some point within a seven- to nine-day period of time.

The development of new moderating strategies that foster inquiry within an asynchronous environment, and the cultivation of impassioned communities of colleagues, are both powerful results of this model, the usefulness of which will continue beyond the scope of any particular netcourse.

PRINCIPLES OF EFFECTIVE MODERATING

Let us now examine the three "principles of effective moderating" that have emerged thus far from our experiences in educating people in the facilitation of online discussion.

PRINCIPLE ONE:
Moderating Takes Place in Both a Professional and a Social Context

Before having any experience with a netcourse or an online working group, many people quite naturally ask themselves one or both of the following questions:

- Will I see any real benefits from participating in a cyber community?
- Can the feeling of community be created online *at all*?

Perhaps these people imagine the apparent solitude of a participant sitting alone in front of a computer at work or in a home office. From our experiences, though, the answer to both of the above questions is "yes!" Community doesn't just happen, however. It takes certain netcourse design criteria and leadership practices to build strong communities. But it can be done — and when it is, results have shown that participants in such effective communities use their course experiences to make real differences in their own professional practices.

Clearly there are social elements and surroundings in face-to-face course sessions or business meetings. We have found that it is essential to foster similar social elements in an online community. The challenge is that the virtual counterparts for social rituals such as greeting one another and chatting informally before getting down to business are not exact replicas of those in the "real" world. Many before us have been searching in the dark of the new medium for a way to create powerful social bonding that feels unaffected and becomes tangible as a real community. Such protocols and rituals are needed at the start of a course or an online forum, and as a continued support for the learning community. An example from the TLC illustrates the importance of the synergy between the social context and the professional context for building an effective online learning community.

The aim of the TLC is to teach participants how to create their own online communities of inquiry learners — i.e., their own netcourses in which students build their own knowledge. The online structure of the TLC acts as a natural model for participants. They build an online course in LearningSpace by means of taking a course that was built with that same courseware. The personal experience better prepares them to design and facilitate their own netcourse communities.

Unsolicited by TLC moderators, one past participant described her experiences in a university-offered, Internet-based course she was taking at the same time she was participating in the TLC. She wrote:

> I'm taking it concurrently with two students in my school; we form a mini study group. The instructor posted a syllabus with homework assignments for each week at the beginning of the term, she amended it once, and each week we hand in homework. Somewhere between a week or two later we get it back. In between, we work with each other or by emailing the instructor, who's very responsive to email. We have had a midterm and expect a final. ... This course has been essentially self-taught, with none of the sense of community that we all want to foster and be part of [here in the TLC].

6

The course model described by this TLC participant — syllabus, weekly homework, and exams with rapid feedback — is very common for online offerings. It appears to be very similar to face-to-face offerings. That the instructor is "very responsive to email," and that students in the course "work with each other," do not mitigate the assessment that the "course has been essentially self taught, with none of the sense of community ... of ... the TLC." In fact, this feeling continues to thrive among TLC graduates today. More than a year later, this same teacher has taught her own netcourse three times. She also volunteers as a mentor "buddy" for new teachers just starting the TLC. Would the same university course, taken face to face, with a very responsive instructor, be described as "essentially self-taught" with no sense of community? Whatever the answer, we do know that online courses like the TLC — which have taken careful steps to support community interaction, beyond merely laying out the syllabus and exam schedules and being attentive to inquiries — reap significant dividends that emerge through participants' achievement and sense of accomplishment.

Additional evidence of the strong community that forms among TLC participants appeared when the TLC participants all met in person for the first time at a VHS conference, after they had completed the TLC and were already teaching their own netcourses. Classmates who had never "met" each other in person were hugging, laughing, and sharing stories like old friends. As one person put it, "This was no awkward meeting of forty strangers coming together for the first time. This was a class reunion!"

One of the most exciting aspects of netcourses is this potential to bring people from around the world together to form close-knit communities of co-learners around areas of professional interest. Our netcourse model demonstrates that people do not need to be physically present with one another to form trusting professional relationships and friendships. But a skilled facilitator is key to the creation of such communities.

PRINCIPLE TWO:
The Style of "Guide on the Side" (vs. "Sage on the Stage") is Most Appropriate for Leading a Virtual Learning Community

Taking the stance of "Guide on the Side" in virtual learning communities proves advantageous for a number of reasons. The most important: Such a pedagogical approach fosters an online culture in which participants take charge of their own learning. As participants react to content, share challenges, teach each other, and learn tangibly by putting into words (discussion postings) their own understandings and clarifications of assumptions, they experiment with and eventually take ownership of new skills and ideas. All along, the "Guide on the Side" serves to focus and deepen the dialogue without getting in the way of participants' development of their own expertise.

A common question early on in an inquiry-based online learning community is, "Where is our leader?" or, "Who's in charge [read *responsible*] here?" Eventually, as owners of their own products and outcomes, participants know not to look outside of themselves for a teacher or an expert. If a moderator can successfully *guide* instead of *giving expert answers*, then learning is maximized as participants are pushed to learn by doing instead of rote copying. At the same time, however, tangents are helpfully cut short.

Staying on the sidelines also offers one additional benefit: There easily can be too much for one person to read and address if a more central "answer person" style emerges. Also, to capitalize on the scalability of excellent course design, it is quite possible that the moderator of the discussion areas may not be the author of the course materials. The same well-crafted course, facilitated by a skillful moderator who is not necessarily an expert in the subjects learned and discussed, can still offer high-quality outcomes to its participants.

Some background. There is a bit of history underlying this particular principle of successful moderating. The rest of this subsection opens up that view for interested readers. We think it's worth understanding because it clarifies why so many online courses are failing, even when the problem does not lie in the course's content or design. So if you're interested in understanding more of this background, read on. Otherwise, go ahead and skip to Principle Three.

The potential for asynchronous interaction among a community of learners, unhindered by geographic location, is very much a reality. Individuals can now log on at low cost from work, school, home, the library, or even their hotel. Master instructors or dialogue leaders from anywhere in the world can collaborate with course design teams that include researchers, scientists, business experts, and experienced online course developers to produce exemplary offerings. But a significant challenge remains: Establishing mechanisms to engage learners' minds directly and collaboratively with the materials. As others who have pioneered this new medium have come to recognize, simply repackaging a lecture-and-discussion-section model of delivery and expecting participants' interest and achievement to automatically follow do not make for the most productive online experience.

Synchronous communication technologies — such as two-way voice and video, real-time chats, and shared applications — are certainly part of modern corporate culture. As part of netcourses, such events might include start-up, group-building, or core decision-making activities and formal presentations. But complex scheduling, demands on technology, bandwidth, and technical support consume considerable resources for a short period of computer-mediated meeting when everyone is present at the same time. That's why The Concord Consortium netcourse model uses a *scheduled asynchronous* format, though judicious use of synchronous forms is occasionally employed for limited purposes. The asynchronous technologies include electronic mail, web-based threaded discussion conferencing, and newsgroups or listservs.

Text-based asynchronous electronic communication is well suited for goal-oriented dialogue and learning environments. No one is left out of a fast-moving conversation or is silenced because he or she is not called upon in the classroom. The reverse is also true, in that the excuse of running out of time as the bell rings is no longer available to participants who are hoping to pass by simply attending class regularly. The act of committing thought to print impresses upon the participant a need for both reflection and clarity. And absence from dialogue, or shallow interaction, shows up quite clearly in threaded text formats.

In fact, web-based threaded discussions can maximize the usefulness of electronic dialogue by giving posts an outline organizational structure. This keeps material in an order related to message *content* rather than *chronology*. Users can follow a conversation much more adeptly than in the context of, for instance, a listserv, for which comments arrive in one's email box as they are sent and relate to any number of main threads, in whatever order people asynchronously visit and post to the discussion; the recipient is then left to organize the conversation in his or her head.

Figure 1 illustrates how a set of discussion threads might appear:

[Previous Main Topic]
Tech issues October * You are here.
.. Attached images
..Working with images: sources of images
.. Thread Maps
.. Getting an emailed URL to work.
.. Tech issues October - What should AOL users do?
....What about AOL users?
...... AOL issues
.... AOL issues for newbies
.... Re: AOL issues for newbies
.... Re: netscape download AOL!!! neat news
[Next Main Topic]

Figure 1.1

Having the freedom to reflect and to craft and recraft a response to a lesson or discussion topic creates more thoughtful discourse than the rushed, spur-of-the-moment contributions participants offer in a face-to-face setting. Participants who are shy or intimidated about speaking in a real-time setting have more opportunity to find their voices in online forums.

A medium that supports learners' ownership of dialogue and their active engagement with content is certainly a good thing. But the question of what form the voice of an instructor or moderator should take on assumes added importance. To make room for individual and collective grappling with ideas, the moderator of the discussion must take a stance that keeps him or her outside the center of the conversation. As the "Guide on the Side," a moderator facilitates the forward movement of the dialogue and helps participants, both individually and collectively, see their own ideas in new combinations and at new levels of significance. This process has been described in the literature as facilitating a community of learners who are engaged in inquiry. Again, learning through inquiry is not a new idea; yet its importance reveals itself through the centrality of inquiry in recent United States public education reform efforts. *The National Science Education Standards* (NSES) describe inquiry in terms of science learning:

Inquiry is central to science learning. When engaging in inquiry, students describe objects and events, ask questions, construct explanations, test those explanations against current scientific knowledge, and communicate their ideas to others. They identify their assumptions, use critical and logical thinking, and consider alternative explanations. In this way, students actively develop their understanding of science by combining scientific knowledge with reasoning and thinking skills. (National Research Council, 1991. Also, see the web site www.nap.edu/readingroom/books/nses/html/overview.html)

In Chapter 10 (Mental Models) of the book *The Fifth Discipline*, author Peter Senge (1990, 192) explores, in the context of team learning in a face-to-face environment, the tension between inquiry and advocacy, and the importance of using inquiry to recognize "leaps of abstraction" that are founded on assumptions or cherished notions in the corporate context. Senge suggests inquiry and reflection as a way to move away from defensive reactions and advocacy of personal positions to an investigation of why these views are held. Dialogue openers like, "Do you see gaps in my reasoning?" or, "How did you arrive at your view?" lead teams to examine freely their own beliefs; they also help team members think clearly about views and the reasons people support them. The "Ladder of Inference" from Senge's book is simply an organizer to help people "identify their assumptions, use critical and logical thinking, and consider alternative explanations," to use the NSES language.

Questions like these and honest dialogue on the issues raised can foster lasting professional growth and learning. The online environment lends itself well to enabling leaders who are accustomed to the role of "Sage on the Stage" to shift to a "Guide on the Side" approach. In a text-based venue, it can be easier to avoid "knee-jerk" actions and reactions because opportunities to reflect, edit, and revise before posting are built in. Facilitators have the luxury of time to craft their interventions into participant-led dialogue, even sharing them among other moderators for feedback before posting.

Indeed, facilitators and participants alike benefit from asynchronous communication technologies. Airtime requires neither quick thinking nor a real-time space in the ongoing discussion. "Interrupting" isn't a 'netiquette issue at all. Teachers who find it hard to employ "wait time" strategies in the classroom will discover that wait time is a natural dimension of an asynchronous threaded discussion.

But moderators can be misled sometimes! The temptation to jump into an online dialogue can be just as great as it is in real-time discussions. Holding back can create a culture that recognizes the benefits to learners who share in the responsibility for teaching and who learn more as a result.

Participants who might feel, at least at first, that no one is "teaching" or leading them might also have to make adjustments in the asynchronous online environment. Eventually, though, they typically discover the power of coconstructing solutions to real or practice problems, encouraged by a style of moderating that is more "guiding" than "leading."

PRINCIPLE THREE:
Online Moderation Is a Craft That Has General Principles and Strategies — That Can Be Learned

Skilled workshop facilitators and instructors bring to their practice myriad skills. They are attuned to hundreds of nonverbal cues and are sensitive to the social context, expectations, and time frames of their product: a well-received workshop or lecture.

But the attention to detail with respect to personal appearance and perceived style, control of voice and intonation, the careful setup of visual field or seating arrangements, and the sequencing and timing of handouts are all absent in asynchronous text-based environments. For many instructors or leaders attempting to make the transition to online forums, the distinct advantages presented by asynchronous communication are difficult to incorporate into their personal and professional styles. Among those advantages are:

- More time for leaders to reflect and to clarify reactions and composition.
- The medium's tendency to force all participants, including leaders, to pre-organize their thoughts.
- The freedom, as leader, to take on, at different times, very different written voice styles, or to carefully articulate alternative interpretations whose depth or subtlety would be lost in the heat of a face-to-face discussion.

Moving from the stance of a traditional instructor or workshop leader to a virtual "Guide on the Side" requires a profound shift in one's thinking and approach. Moderators must learn new strategies that are appropriate to the online venue, and, through continued practice, study the range of their effects.

Also, we have found that even talented online moderators rely on one, or at most very few, styles or modes of interaction with participants in a dialogue. Later chapters in this book outline a set of critical thinking strategies (Chapter 7) and a palette of voices (Chapter 5) and tones (Chapter 6) that you may use as a moderator to optimize participants' learning opportunities in online discussions. The craft of virtual moderating can be learned, much like the crafts of running a fine workshop or presenting an exemplary lecture (although the skills and strategies for each are quite different).

One of the most difficult skills — or perhaps mindsets — that practitioners who are new to the "Guide on the Side" approach report is gaining a fresh sense of the word "reflection." Participants' comments, not their own, provide the scaffolding for further learning. In one strategy, for example, the moderator gleans from various posts some insights to generate further dialogue or to juxtapose and compare for deeper meaning or application. The goal is to help learners as their *own* thinking evolves. The moderator's insights or experiences are not central, and they may even compete with the process.

INTEC moderators, while honing their skills in a discussion area set aside just for their own use, have commented that they felt at first considerable uneasiness and frustration with this new kind of process. Their postings contained very few of their own ideas, and they felt "up to their ears" in the ideas of others: "Sometimes I feel a bit like a plagiarist. Is what we are doing ... a kind of stealing?"

Moderators' discomfort with working intimately with others' thoughts in a dialogue can certainly be real. They can and do ask themselves, "Where am I in this mix?" There is a strong tendency to "hop in" with a practiced commentary or connection made from professional experience or one's own training. On occasion, such interventions may be useful if the group is "wallowing in the shallows" or meandering far from the track. In general, however, the craft of holding up participants' *own* thoughts in a clearer or more layered form can achieve much longer-lasting personal development than the "added gem" of a comment.

A metaphor INTEC moderators find useful in this context is "Moderator as Thief." The thieving moderator in this analogy breaks into a discussion and, instead of removing objects, uncovers something of value. Thus, the kind of "thief" we're speaking of actually leaves something behind. It may be comments, or tangential material that contains key insights, much like opening a forgotten book to a particularly relevant page. Parallels, congruencies, or incongruencies within individual or group approaches are brought to the center of the room. A sense of ownership of the ideas is essential to progress; ownership of ideas is best retained by the dialogue participants.

A model for interaction that stresses creativity and insight constrained by a limited set of effective protocols is not new. Counseling strategies used by psychologists, social workers, or conflict managers operate at a professional level within similar frameworks. The set of critical thinking strategies and the palette of voices and tones set out in later chapters offer tools that keep you, the moderator, at a much-needed distance from the ideas in a dialogue, and help you reframe or reveal components or implications to those that authored those ideas.

At first, consciously deciding to communicate using a voice that may not seem like your own can feel unnatural. Professors are accustomed to the role of *conceptual facilitator*. Those with training in social or behavioral science naturally compose as *mediators* or *conveyors of the value of multiple perspectives*. Writers author as *storytellers* or *personal muses*. All of these approaches and others are needed for effective moderation as a "Guide on the Side." Facilitators, supported by training, can capture the advantages offered by an asynchronous text-based medium to foster critical reflection and individual and collaborative learning that rivals — and may even exceed — traditional settings for instruction.

THE NEW LANDSCAPE

The rapid evolution of possibilities for online courses means that new principles for netcourse design and facilitation will continue to emerge as the potential of the technologies grows. Chapter 2 delves more deeply into the new functions of the virtual moderator and examines how these functions might be achieved with some training and collegial support.

Chapter Two

NEGOTIATING SPACE: FORMS OF DIALOGUE AND GOALS OF MODERATING

■■■■■■■■ Many factors influence the form, expectations, and purposes for online professional dialogue. Among them: goals, institutional guidelines, facilitator and participant expectations for individual or collaborative work, content and layout, and interface and software capability. (Note: Issues relating to interface, layout, content, and institutional setting lie beyond the scope of this book.) As such, at the start of any such endeavor, participants and facilitators naturally experiment with and negotiate the meanings and expectations in their new virtual discussion area(s). They explore how the virtual space can and will support the goals and objectives of the community. It can take awhile for participants to gain understanding of and confidence in the function and purpose of the shared dialogue spaces.

Guidance from a moderator who can essentially "see" what's going on in a dialogue and light the way forward is essential for progress. This chapter offers a breakdown of the dialogical elements we've found helpful in viewing and interpreting text-based actions of both discussion moderators and participants. Once you, the moderator, can analyze online activity using such lenses, it's much easier to bring about progress toward community goals. You'll serve an invaluable role when you can capably utilize constructive elements of a dialogue to sharpen the focus and point to areas in which further dialogue is needed to generate growth and learning.

Initial postings by both experienced and novice online learners are often characterized by comments that are disconnected from either an assignment or from each other's postings. In a more constructive light, these disjointed notes can be viewed as essential experiments with the course design, the interface, or the "sound" of a participant's own voice online. As the moderator, you can work within the parameters of design and institutional frame to clarify expectations, roles, uses of virtual spaces to build a general sense of direction and comfort with common goals, expected outcomes, and the means to achieve those goals.

The most difficult part of negotiating online space, for all parties, lies in the successive transformation from initial, *ice-breaking* discourse — which is largely disconnected to future course content — to a phase that may be termed *wallowing in the shallows*, and then on to dialogue that can be called *reasoned discourse*. Initial tasks commonly include introductions, chats, group or team formations, the setting of expectations, the expression of personal interests, or springboard activities. In such discussion threads, participants build sufficient sense of community and shared vision to begin more substantive interactions. Participants who progress beyond the first phase have a sense of group goals as well as some facility with the interface.

But a vision of how the dialogue areas connect to individual and collaborative learning may take longer to fully develop. By interacting with posts individually and collectively, you the moderator model constructive commentary, and you facilitate your learners as they move to active participation in sustained, reflective, reasoned discourse about content. This most useful phase of dialogue becomes the centerpiece around which real learning and growth can occur.

Sometimes for individuals, or even whole groups, the negotiating phase of understanding the space does not stabilize, all the pieces don't quite fall together, and the "shallows" are occupied for a much longer time than is useful — perhaps even for the duration of the course. This common frustration for online moderators is an experience once shared by the authors of this book — and it motivates us to write about what we have found can move discussion beyond the "shallows" to the richer kind of dialogue that asynchronous text-based discussion areas make possible.

By taking a step back and surveying the landscape of online discussions, you can begin to move forward from being stuck in less-than-constructive (even pointless) dialogue. Recognizing the forms a dialogue can take serves to explain the phenomenon in a general way and helps you focus on how to move the community forward, leave the "shallows," and enter the exciting depths where real learning happens.

FORMS OF DIALOGUE

The classic literature on dialogue is vast, and it includes classification schemas based on linguistic, logical, or dialectical patterns. Through our work with VHS and INTEC, we have found a simple and effective categorization schema that you can use as a moderator to assist participants through what is, for some, a difficult and awkward transition to learning online.

From theoretical work on critical thinking in the last decade by Paul (1990), Lippman (1991), and Matthies (1996), and from work on dialogue in the corporate arena by Drucker (1988) and Peters and Waterman (1988), we identify, based on their purpose, the three general forms of dialogue: *social dialogue, argumentative dialogue,* and *pragmatic dialogue.* We describe these types of dialogue and their use below.

The categories serve as both a diagnostic and a prescriptive framework to help you analyze posts and then plan interventions that will effectively promote active, collaborative, and focused reflection among members of the learning community. The broad categories of social, argumentative, and pragmatic dialogue tell you which elements of participants' posts have potential to generate and continue reasoned discourse. In your own postings, you can then emphasize these aspects of participants' postings.

Any individual posting can contain all three forms of dialogue. As moderator, you identify the elements and associate them with the purposes of each form in support of the reflective dialogue sought by the group. The elements of communication can reveal motivation, much as do the more familiar classroom exchanges in which instructors see hand or facial gestures, spot shifts in body poses or eye movements, or perceive different inflections in tone. If an entry is purely *social,* for example, you can direct the respondent to the appropriate forum (for instance, a "Water Cooler" discussion thread or another separate area) or highlight elements that lead to deeper reflection. If the entry is *argumentative,* you may select elements of the post and offer strategies for commentary that redirect the discussion away from defending positions and toward exploration of reasoning.

Your goal as moderator is to cultivate dialogue with an increasingly pragmatic purpose.

Let's explore these forms of dialogue further, and then examine how you may use each to focus participants' dialogue on learning goals.

Social Dialogue

When we first opened the TLC, we hadn't thought of how basic and necessary it would be to provide a virtual space for *social dialogue* or simple chitchat — news like someone just signing papers on their first home or having a new grandchild. We discovered quickly how critical it is! Comments unrelated to the course kept getting sprinkled into the "Course Room" discussion area, where course content was supposed to be the focus. And once someone said they'd had their first grandchild, others had to post at least a "congratulations," if not a "Hey, I just had my sixth!" or a "That's my daughter's name, too."

What's a good moderator to do? Chat certainly fosters an important sense of belonging, and that is an essential step in establishing a learning community. But just like "talking in class," it's distracting when the focus is supposed to be elsewhere. So we quickly created a separate discussion area, the "Water Cooler," and pointed out its purpose.

Now, the TLC always begins with social "icebreakers" in the Course Room discussion area. Then, two or three weeks into the course, we use an assignment to transition social dialogue away from the content discussion areas and into the Water Cooler area. Participants are assigned to visit the existing Water Cooler to check out who's there. Once they've visited the Water Cooler, it's easier to maintain appropriate focus in the Course Room.

In entering such social areas, participants can leave behind serious discussion and enter a space to just "hang out" with their peers, either asynchronously or synchronously. Conversations can assume intimate or personal dimensions. It seems that some participants can share more intimately than might be possible with the group of professionals whom they see every day. The fact that strangers, who have never met face to face, feel comfortable sharing very personal and meaningful accounts of their daily lives underscores the need such personal spaces fulfill. In the TLC Water

Cooler, teachers discuss everything from family to the future of distance learning, from vacations to software packages, from favorite sports teams to art censorship in the schools.

Conversations that begin with a purely social frame can also naturally ease into discussions that have significant impact on the exploration of course content. One TLC participant described her experiences in the Water Cooler area as follows:

> I do think that both I (and my students) learn as much from fooling around on the 'Net as we do when involved in "serious business." It seems to me that one thing we've all seen is that "bonding" happens more easily in the Water Cooler than on the assignments. And I've been thinking of all kinds of ways to use a similar space to accomplish the goal of bonding in my AP 'Netclass. Which only makes sense, since that is exactly what I do in my "real" AP class (and more there than in my "regular courses").

Though presented in the Water Cooler, the TLC social arena, this response indicates a familiarity with the medium of dialogue that goes beyond simple social interaction. This teacher uses observation and personal reflection to invite substantive discussion about the "bonding" she has experienced in the Water Cooler, and she muses about the potential for her own AP netcourse. Thus, the goals of the community-building assignments have been attained: She has moved beyond social dialogue and shallow discussions about terms and negotiating the meaning of assignments and spaces. She has also developed a confidence and a personal voice, as shown in this communication.

As moderator, you may then elect to collect quotations from other responses — consciously including quotes from participants who are still in disjointed or "shallow" phases, or who are experimenting with their own online voice — and build a post in the main area exploring parallels and the value of "bonding" in virtual and face-to-face groups. In constructing such a post, you build bridges that help participants over the necessary transition to reasoned discourse.

A significant benefit of the trust initiated and supported by rich interactions in social forums is the potential spillover of willingness to engage in open communication in content assignments. One teacher noted that he has never seen the level of intimacy and personal expression in students' writing that he's seen in his VHS netcourse. He believes students feel more comfortable expressing themselves and going out on a creative limb with strangers or in a text-based community.

Beyond communications in spaces designed for social interaction, social dialogue will continue to be evident in many responses in task-oriented areas. These social pieces are what might be termed the "ritual elements of dialogue," which include discussion of weather or the drive to work, short personal musings, daily interactions with participants, or other discussion "openers." These elements commonly provide a frame or context for moving to interaction with ideas on a deeper level. Participants often give clues to their opinions, or perhaps evidence of assumptions or beliefs, through what may be seemingly unrelated social dialogue elements:

> ### MESSAGE SUBJECT: Re: Educational Reform
>
> An empty discussion area is a forbidding place ... but comment I must. I just looked at the week 4 & 5 assignments, and my gut sank. Why? Well, first I need to tell you I haven't yet done the reading; I will in the next few days. Then I'll come back and probably revise this posting (if I haven't been run out of the group by instructors or colleagues). But in the last few months, thanks to another class and a plethora of ill-conceived reform efforts in and around my school, I've been thinking and reading lots about change.

This participant, in his introduction, offers some excuses for being out of the dialogue. Yet he feels sufficiently supported by the TLC moderators to be honest and even humorous about his late and unprepared entry. This paragraph is followed by thoughtful and well-articulated sparring with some of the main ideas and purposes of educational reform, which he then relates to the "ill-conceived" efforts at his school. Empty areas do pose challenges for participants and for you as the facilitator. This participant boldly posted a thoughtful entry triggered by what seems to be a hot button: "educational reform." If you were the moderator here, you could then identify specific assumptions and parallels in the course readings to make concrete any concerns about their relevancy and purpose.

In the following example from an INTEC assignment area, a participant reveals his level of understanding of the course goals, as well as his own expectations. The respondent had completed the *ramping up* (introductory) activities, in which the participants had posted personal introductions, read articles and commented on them, and mastered the interface. The assignment posed specific questions about an assigned article and invited learners to try out some modeling software:

MESSAGE SUBJECT: Activity 1 — Building a Model

I've found the space to write in at last. This is [the author's name]. I teach 7th grade science in a middle school in western Pennsylvania. I really liked the readings. They seemed relevant to my classroom and our curriculum. I don't quite understand what is going on with the assignments and this discussion space. There doesn't seem to be a lot of instruction going on. I do like reading people's comments. Well, I'm going to work in the environmental simulation tomorrow.

This post is strongly social in its intention. It seems motivated by a desire to post something, as required by the assignment. The participant has moved beyond initial experimentation, and he displays some mastery of the interface. He does not see how changing the "message subject" header can clarify communication. He is certainly wallowing in the shallows with regard to the goals of the course and an understanding of the purpose of the discussion space.

A tale about a geometry teacher attempting to implement new instructional methods captures the thought pattern the writer exhibits. "A geometry student leans over and tells a friend, 'This new math teacher doesn't know much about geometry. She just put up $a^2 + b^2 = c^2$ for right triangles and asked us to prove it.'" For the writer above, instruction and learning are things that happen to him, not processes in which he must actively engage. His expectations for "instruction," derived perhaps from lecture delivery systems or personal tutoring, are in conflict with the general design of an online course, in which participants are expected to interact with material and each other within the rich frame set by the assignment. His approving comments on the readings and their relevance serve no purpose other than social chitchat; he engages neither their content nor that of any of the other contributors. He anticipates the segment of the assignment regarding learning from interaction with the computer simulation, but he puts it off to another time.

Entries like this one are very common early on. The writer's flawed conception of the discussion space and the expectations for participants survived well past its usefulness to him and to others. As the facilitator in such a case, recognizing the source of the problem, you might invite this participant (through a personal email) to contribute insights on why the articles were agreeable and to solicit reactions to running the model. Publicly, you may juxtapose this affirmation with other posts that are more critical and invite comments about the simulations. To draw this particular participant and others into substantive discussion, you might even highlight his name in the post. The goal of such a posting is to move participants from contributing messages that have a social context to actively engaging with the content material.

Sometimes social text unintentionally sounds patronizing. When we suggest you initiate personal email as the moderator, not just any message will work. Be aware that your postings and emails are transparent when you apply a social "cover" to an evaluative comment or question. Even if you intend your commentary to be benign, helpful, or caring, it may not be perceived that way because you're in a position of authority. For example, the simple query, "How are you doing?" can readily be interpreted as part of a policing or information-gathering sortie by a boss looking over a participant's shoulder.

It's helpful, then, to distinguish between *authoritarian* and *authoritative* communications. The authoritarian comment has the most potential to adversely affect the healthy climate for open dialogue. "Authoritarian" denotes control or directiveness. To the query, "How are you doing?," a participant sensing an authoritarian purpose in the question may think, "Have I posted enough? Are my entries of sufficient quality?" or "What is it he really wants to know? It may be time for excuses." If you send the note via email outside the discussion area, the recipient may well wonder if others are also singled out for such unsolicited attention.

If you feel you must contact a participant as part of your "keeping-up-the-pace" function, it may be helpful to frame your message as social, to the degree possible, without falling into a patronizing, authoritarian stance. You can replace your "How are you doing?" comment with something like "How can we help?" preceding it with some conversation about your own personal problems with the ISP or other hardware issues. These communications empower participants whose commitment lags for technical or other reasons, and they may give the participants a pretext to jump back on board. Both the phrasing and equalizing context shift the question to an *authoritative* context in which you the facilitator are seen as a legitimate source of assistance.

Authoritative elements, from participants, you the moderator, or other sources (for instance, in INTEC, we bring "Field Experts" to the online discussion at appropriate times), serve as graceful introductions of valued insights. If you cite their expertise and credibility, you honor your participants and give context to their contributions. This strategy is also useful for opening up lines of thought, especially if you treat it as scaffolding for further investigation of value or sources of information and not as a means to control or limit a line of thought. Conversely, authoritative elements that emerge as part of a dialogue whose purpose is argumentative become authoritarian.

Argumentative Dialogue

Dialogue whose purpose is *argumentative* is familiar to all of us who have been in the place where we can't stop ourselves from displays of rhetorical power, scoring points in our own eyes while sometimes even impressing others. Strongly advocating a particular view involves the use of impassioned presentation and pointers to evidence, with the goal of changing listeners' minds. Certainly participants may become engaged in taking and defending positions, but the central question for a dialogue that features inquiry is, what is gained?

Reasoned discourse, on the other hand, is a process that challenges participants to move beyond debate to honor multiple perspectives by sorting through tensions and seeking deeper common meaning or outcomes. In constructive group work for learning and growth, there need not be winners and losers. Achievement of high quality in specified common outcomes is more important than the winners and losers of internal debate. The value of a participant's contribution is demonstrated by its usefulness toward the goals of the community.

It's important for participants to feel unconstrained and supported as they attempt to go beyond commitment to an idea or assumption and examine their long-held beliefs. An exchange whose form may initially be argumentative can transition to a dialogue that values inquiry — if participants and you the moderator maintain a stance in which ideas are examined openly and honestly with questions like, "Can you help me to think more clearly about these issues?" or, "Can you help me think more clearly about what I've just stated? I find this approach very attractive but don't really find it convincing." As moderator, you can model moving away from defending individual positions and toward an inquiry into why beliefs or assumptions are held to be valid.

The authoritative stance can, unfortunately, become authoritarian if it enters strongly and often into such dialogue, bringing with it the capacity to circumvent further insight, albeit unintentionally. All disciplines have authorities; the champions of one set of views or another. The challenge for you the moderator is not identifying authoritarian elements in a dialogue, but moving the conceptual frame away from a debate about "sides" to a reasoned examination of the sources of belief. Challenging someone's assertions based on personal experience or appeals to revered sources taken at face value often leads to defensive reactions and lengthy verbal jousting — something we've called *argumentative dialogue* — and not pragmatic, reasoned dialogue. Participants thus disengage, and dialogue short circuits. If you the moderator openly examine the "why" of statements and their relevance to current issues or content, you build a ramp to more fertile explorations.

Softer forms of argumentative dialogue.

Benign advocacy. It's tempting for you or a participant to persuade, to advocate, as a means of ostensibly helping. But there's a downside to such an effort. As noted by Senge (1990), there's a fundamental tension between advocacy and its potential to effectively control dialogue and prevent further insight. Advocacy is essentially a way to market something. That something can be an idea, a vision, a service, or a widget and its use. There's nothing fundamentally wrong with such marketing. However, as Senge notes, the problem surfaces when one is trying to inquire openly about issues and potential approaches to the topic at hand. Advocacy may close down avenues of productive thinking. So as the facilitator of an online learning community, you must be aware of potential interpretations of advocacy and control seeking, so that you can create and maintain a spirit of open dialogue.

Appeal against progress. Dialogue whose purpose is argumentative need not be solely of the "verbal joust" variety. A participant may use an argumentative entry to slow down or distance himself or herself from the discussion by invoking an image of overload of one type or another ("I'm too busy," "This is too new," "This is too complex," etc.). In this quote from an INTEC dialogue, for instance, a teacher remarks on her efforts to learn a new software application:

> I really need a lot more time to do this assignment any justice. I really don't have the time to read through this in enough detail so that I feel comfortable enough to use it with my students. I need an entire day to sit and read through this and work out my problems without having to worry about the other items going on in my classroom, especially considering that our semester is up and I have tons of grading to do, due to missing seven days of school. I feel like this is a good program, but I would like to have this over a summer or a long break, so that I could concentrate on this and this alone. Do any of you feel like this as well? Right now I am extremely overwhelmed and don't feel like I am really doing enough work on this to give it a real shot. Any comments would be welcome.

The opening sentences present a social context — a hard-pressed classroom teacher. They offer insights to the moderator on the participant's motivation and her perceptions of what needs to be done. The phrase "extremely overwhelmed" echoed in several subsequent responses to this post. The sense of these postings was "Whoa! Stop! This stuff is good, but I don't have time to do it!" Although the participant recognized the value of the material, she had difficulty taking a longer view.

Any course that attempts to build capacity or level of skill and understanding is bound to encounter responses of this sort. Time is put up as a barrier to improvement, and it is inherently difficult to challenge another person's time availability. We are all the best authority on our own time. There are several critical thinking strategies, described in Chapter 7, available to you as a moderator to help you deal with blocks to exploration, which may include perceptions of what is possible.

Importantly, the last sentence of this participant's post invites comment. She had sufficient trust in the community to do this venting, and she openly solicited suggestions. The moderator can thus open the lines of engagement in alternative views.

Passive form of argumentative dialogue. The argumentative stance can also hide behind a more subtle format — another use of advocacy. Advocating a certain view can serve as a type of passive resistance to change. Once the dialogue is perceived as a place to take positions and defend them, outcomes become limited to what is "given," and knowledge coconstruction is limited to what participants already understand. An INTEC participant, for example, writes:

> I have learned to read all articles regarding the teaching of mathematics with a skeptical view. First, you must realize that the author is trying to get a point across and therefore goes too much to one side of an issue. Second and last, every teacher knows that balance is the key. The subject matter doesn't even matter. Too much of one method is never beneficial, for teacher or student. A successful teacher varies methods and keeps changing and improving his/her lessons. So what if an author seems to support one method versus another. They got you to think about what you do in the classroom and for that they are successful!

There is certainly nothing off track about voicing a healthy sense of skepticism. Certainly, bringing ideas into question is central to any process of inquiry, scientific or otherwise. The writer here posits that "balance is the key," but the key to what? What precisely is to be balanced? The posting is a bit of a closed door; the respondent does not engage the productive element: "Think[ing] about what you do in a classroom." Resistance to methods or presentations that are perceived as argumentative or perhaps rhetorical is evident.

If you were the moderator in this case, you could further the discussion by urging the writer to talk more specifically about what she believes really works and why. Such an approach will push participants to move away from simple platitudes.

Pragmatic Dialogue

Pragmatic dialogue is reasoned discourse whose process serves ends beyond the dialogue itself. Its goal is not to persuade, but rather to inquire and to use the dialogue to inform participants in both a collective and an individual way so that they exchange varied thoughts, ideas, and approaches to whatever subject matter they're considering.

Pragmatic dialogue (Rorty 1979, Matthies 1996, Lippman 1991) differs from social and argumentative forms of dialogue in three essential ways:

- There's a specific goal or task for the dialogue and a limited time frame for its accomplishment.
- Personal investment in ideas is relaxed in favor of a group investment in achieving progress or forward movement of the dialogue. A person's most firmly held ideas are open for discussion.
- Given constraints of time and personal resources, many ideas cannot be pursued. Pragmatic dialogue is characterized by what can be called a "collective conceptual triage." Participants, actively facilitated by you the moderator, identify very attractive but potentially tangential or divergent ideas and concentrate instead on those that hold promise of yielding results that will add to achieving the goals of the collaboration.

Participants in pragmatic dialogue value the tough questions and the importance of the unknown. They don't assume the validity of generalizations, beliefs, or statements of fact; instead, they're honestly open to genuinely questioning. They welcome both confirming and challenging data and interpretations. The goal is not encouragement of tedious or perhaps comic hair splitting, but rather an open examination of why claims, assertions, or beliefs are held. A participant can ask, "What is the relationship to any supporting data?" not as a challenge, but as part of an effort to help everyone think clearly about their reasoning. Pragmatic dialogue strongly supports inquiry and reflective thinking. You the moderator and your group should be genuinely interested in finding reasons for your views and assessing the strengths and weaknesses of those reasons.

Support and capacity for pragmatic dialogue do not emerge overnight. People are accustomed to advocating their personal views of "correct" solutions, or parrying others' equally resolute attempts to convince. Thus, progress toward opening and sustaining pragmatic dialogue comes slowly. New aspects of long-held beliefs are revealed over time so that new ways of seeing develop. These are the fruits of the process of inquiry.

Goals of moderating in a pragmatic dialogue. Though social and argumentative forms of dialogue are present in most discourse, the intention of pragmatic dialogue — time-limited, product-driven dialogue that is critically sensitive to collaboration and the use of each participant's personal resources — provides a supportive framework for the goal-directed conversations needed in online courses or project work groups. Specific goals related to content or process will certainly be critical in introductory sessions or assignments for participants. The following are among those goals.

Goal one: Building community. Cultivating a social environment and extended interaction within an online discussion group requires particular care if the community is to be perceived by participants as more than just a string of emails or postings. As moderator, you need to build a climate that will foster professional learning or collaboration by crafting communications that support a sense of safety in the discussion areas.

Clearly all learning communities, online and off, share this concern at some level. In cultivating pragmatic dialogue, maintaining a sense of safety is particularly pressing. Inquiry is an intimate process. The expectation is that participants should distance themselves from their own thoughts and beliefs in order to design the best product possible or engage in the greatest possible learning. In online or classroom settings, many people feel some level of discomfort with this inquiry process. Simply advocating for what one feels or knows to be true is much easier. A process that involves inquiry confronts the unknown and relies on personal or collective resources to resolve questions. The online environment in which inquiry can flourish is gradually built by collaborative and collective contributions. Such collaborative efforts are likely to result in better outcomes, designs, practices, or products.

Doing any inquiry at all involves an additional factor: risk taking. In the process of inquiry, one often feels unsure or uneasy, at least to some extent. The clarity of the goal, its meaning or relevance, the adequacy of tools, or personal skill in using new tools are all likely to come into question at one time or another. Participants must feel safe to take intellectual risks that can lead to new ways of seeing and new discoveries. They will rely on you the moderator to foster an environment in which they feel safe to express themselves openly and work through their personal and conceptual uncertainty.

Goal two: Supporting a culture of respect. Participants should feel that what they say matters and is valued by the other members of the community. This cultivation of respect, seen as an extension of civility to an

Internet environment, is certainly not new. In moderating for inquiry, with its concern for both openness and uncertainty, an atmosphere of respect takes on added value. In the process of inquiry, individuals may hold up their own beliefs, or perhaps beliefs or assumptions they do not personally espouse, for careful examination. Individuals must feel that, in this process, they are respected and valued for contributing to the productive discussion of the online community.

Goal three: Cultivating reasoned discourse. The central goal of moderating pragmatic dialogue is supporting the intellectual content of the online community. That support may take several forms.

As moderator, you're responsible for maintaining a forward direction of the dialogue. Its context — perhaps an academic course, a project, or a community service forum — defines the goals of such a dialogue. Informed by the problems or goals of the discussion, you must focus emerging ideas and juxtapose emerging tensions. Participants then sense forward direction in the form of greater clarity, richer content or context, and deeper personal vision of or engagement with the goals of the course through the process of inquiry.

As moderator you should, by omission in commentary or redirection, identify tangential lines of thought that may not, in the short term, contribute to deepening the discussion. In supporting inquiry as a "Guide on the Side," you cannot be scared of guiding. Inquiry does not just happen; all ideas are not equally productive. However, tangential ideas are contributed for a reason, and they can become an important source of comparison or alternative viewpoints later in a discussion. Weaving elements of these seemingly discarded pieces back into the dialogue at a later time as springboards for new reflection is an important function of capable moderating toward specific goals.

Cultivating a sense of ownership over the central elements of discourse is also essential to supporting inquiry. "Owning the questions" is another way to capture the idea. Participants should feel that their ideas are defining the direction of the dialogue. As moderator, you should make explicit connections between participants' responses and the tasks or goals of the dialogue. Though one of the main tools for moderating is asking questions, you must also pay careful attention to "whose question is being asked?" If, as moderator, you initiate too many lines of questioning, the power balance of the dialogue shifts and any chance for genuine inquiry suffers. Occupying a central place in the dialogue and asking or formulating the driving questions, or putting up flurries of questions, puts you unduly in charge as moderator. Repeating, clarifying, restating, juxtaposing, extending, and contrasting issues and important lines of questioning are more productive tasks for you as you attempt to foster pragmatic dialogue.

Once you're clear on the form each posting represents — social, argumentative, or pragmatic — you can more easily analyze how best to intervene in an active discussion. The tools and strategies you can use to accomplish the goals of moderating in support of specific production targets or content goals are addressed in the remainder of this book.

Chapter Three

■ ■ ■ ■ ■ ■ ■ ■ ■

KEY
FACILITATOR ROLES

■■■■■■■■■ Whatever challenges motivate you to read this book, it's likely that a part of your professional position is or soon will be leading an online group in a goal-oriented discussion area. The roles you have as a facilitator of online professional dialogue will vary widely and may shift in emphasis with each new group of participants.

Yet there are some basic facilitation skills that any group leader must have to function successfully. Among them: Making participants feel welcome and safe, and modeling the use of the virtual medium to minimize miscommunication. Our experience with INTEC and the TLC has helped us clarify the essential skills that will enhance your success as a facilitator in this critical role.

In this chapter we've divided your role as moderator into three functional categories:

- "Guide on the Side"
- Instructor or project leader
- Group process facilitator

There are additional roles you might take on, but they vary and aren't as directly related to the moderating task.

Here we provide a window into life in the virtual world by supporting much of what we describe with actual examples from our netcourse discussion areas. Pairing our previous conceptions of your role as facilitator with such a tour will be helpful and clarifying, especially if you're just getting started in this new world.

THE FACILITATOR AS "GUIDE ON THE SIDE"

We've met many instructors experimenting with online courses who report being overwhelmed with enrollments as small as ten or twelve, because they end up in email conversations with each participant. "It's like having unlimited office hours," comments one teacher. Their model, which places the teacher in the center of numerous private conversations, is not feasible, nor is it necessarily good teaching (see Figure 3.1).

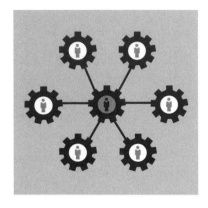

Figure 3.1

When the instructor is the focal point
of all communication, teaching is
cumbersome and less productive.

Figure 3.2

Using the seminar model, the facilitator
supports learning and communication
among the participants themselves.

Our model is more like a seminar in which a team of experts determines the topic and activities. Meanwhile, the course moderators encourage substantive interactions among the participants by monitoring and shaping conversations with targeted interventions, and by refraining from extensive direct interaction (see Figure 3.2).

We call the carefully crafted interactions of the moderator in this model *interventions* to emphasize the difference between a leader on the side-lines and one playing a more central role. Common forms of interaction that can be communicated in seconds in a classroom or meeting — e.g., a nod of approval or a "mmm hmm" of agreement used by a facilitator as she transitions from the point one participant made to signal another participant that it's his turn to speak — cannot be readily accomplished in the online format. Some instructors have attempted to respond to every student posting with confirming feedback. But online, problems immediately arise.

For instance, in the shifting environment of real-time dialogue, appropriate comments can be confirmed and incorrect information may either be passed over or corrected or skirted in favor of comments that move the discussion forward. A capable discussion leader can synthesize where a group has been going at appropriate intervals, helping everyone to refocus on the information that points forward. It isn't always done effectively, but most of us are familiar with live facilitation that easily achieves or orchestrates forward movement in a dialogue.

Online, things are different. Postings are frozen in asynchronous time to appear "forever" in the text-based discussion areas. Comments may be scrutinized over and over again, and they don't fade away as voice-based contributions in a live setting inevitably will. Correcting a participant or shifting the focus of the dialogue toward the goals of the course or discussion can be done and is still needed, but the format calls for a different approach. A virtual nod to confirm each comment has the potential to set up a culture where an approval or disapproval after each posting is expected. In such a scenario, you the facilitator effectively lock yourself out of further communications, as participants are likely to skip over your comments.

One netcourse facilitator describes why the essential shift to "Guide on the Side" can indeed take place when the Internet becomes the classroom:

> There are a number of reasons for the "Sage on the Stage" being such a dominant model for the organization of the classroom. The most quaint probably dates from the Middle Ages — a time when books were scarce and hard and expensive to come by. But one concern that consciously or unconsciously pushes many in the sage direction is no doubt the matter of maintaining order. The logic of the "Sage on the Stage" in this regard is obvious. It may also be a weak excuse for doing the usual. A revolutionary aspect of the technological underpinnings of netcourses is that, in a certain respect, everyone can speak at once — everyone can say what they want, about what they want, when they want — and the order of the group, the order of the classroom, is not necessarily disturbed. This fact should lead teachers who are

thinking of developing netcourses to stop and seriously think about how they are going to go about doing it. The order issue may have joined that of the scarcity of books as a quaint throwback to earlier times.

Common concerns among teachers who are moving to an inquiry-based educational approach often relate to maintaining order (both an ordered course plan and a studious environment) in the classroom. Another frequent concern: Many teachers fear opening themselves up to students' questions that call for knowledge outside the teachers' own expertise. But with Internet access, experts and current information can be at the fingertips of both Internet-savvy teachers and students. Not only does this new factor support teachers moving to new methods, but it is also a powerful incentive for all teachers with Internet (information) access in their classrooms to rethink their roles. Will teachers be able to support students as expert information brokers in twenty-first-century classrooms — modeling how to sort through seemingly infinite resources to target those that are most useful, current, and credible? It is a new and likely difficult shift for today's cadre of teachers, who joined the ranks because their interests and skills were a match for the now "quaint" center-stage teacher image of yesteryear (yesterday!).

We have found that the text-based threaded discussion venue of a netcourse actually makes this juxtaposition of roles easier to achieve in comparison with a face-to-face context. In an asynchronous environment, it's less remarkable that the course "leader" is not positioned in the "center" — either as a focus for speakers or physically in the front of a classroom. From the sidelines, you the online leader can play a powerful role by supporting others in their learning. Gradual forward movement toward learning goals or product outcomes among participants can be achieved using a few targeted interventions into the dialogue, given that you have a repertoire of skills and are able to practice using them.

First, you're challenged to operate as a co-learner who avoids lecturing and instead guides others to deeper insights by identifying and highlighting important points in the course work and discussion comments for everyone to view. The ability to make thoughtful replies to content is, of course, a necessary skill for all teachers and facilitators. But in the online environment, carefully articulated written responses are fundamental —

the student has no other way to receive feedback and encouragement from you because there are no face-to-face interactions. Instead, you can push the thinking of the group with interventions that sharpen the focus.

We've also found that different kinds of courses bring out different aspects of sideline leadership. In INTEC, where participants are moving to a conceptual understanding of inquiry in the classroom, interventions are targeted at that conceptual level. In the TLC, where participants are learning to use database software and develop their skill at netcourse design, the feedback is more direct and grounded in the details. However, both types of course content and goals benefit from the "Guide on the Side" approach.

Moving Participants to a New Conceptual Level

Skilled facilitators of inquiry are naturally geared toward an apparently vague or open stance in discussion activities. Their goals are to focus and deepen the thinking of participants, individually or as a group, without shutting down the inquiring work of the participants themselves.

On the one hand, you can work as a facilitator with the tools of advanced electronic communication. These include rules of 'Netiquette (Internet etiquette), strategies for voice and tone (described in depth in Chapters 5 and 6, respectively), and an approach that builds community by your contributing to the dialogue as a colearner rather than an expert. On the other hand, you must take full advantage of the opportunities of asynchronous dialogue in order to optimize group outcomes. What follows are some specific strategies we've found useful and effective for doing just that.

Avoid publicly praising participants. It will be tempting for you to make approving statements right in the discussion areas when participants make excellent points or post other contributions that support further dialogue. In particular, this can happen early on in the course, or during times when the dialogue is lagging. We have found, however, that such posts actually do the opposite of what you intend: They shut down further dialogue! Perhaps other participants reading your approving words think, "OK, that's what he/she wanted, I don't need to add more."

Instead, as a facilitator you can foster more of what you seek by highlighting comments that are on track. You can choose two or three pertinent points from the postings of a number of participants in a discussion, weave them together, and then use a question to shift the view. That way, you challenge the participants to dig deeper. We call the phrases you cite dialogue elements, and we challenge our moderators to work with a few in each intervention they make.

Draw upon elements that are already in the dialogue to light the way forward. If, as moderator, you hope to stay out of the middle of the dialogue, there is one critical skill you must develop: Identifying comments or phrases, already posted in the dialogue, that can serve as bridges to the next level of understanding for the group.

Surprisingly, the most useful participant quotes are not always the ones that contain "right answers." Some wrong paths can be the best illuminators of a better way to go. By choosing authentic dialogue elements or those that offer clarification because of what they're missing, you in effect provide positive feedback — albeit indirectly — to all of the participants whose posts you've cited. And in a way, you get participants to focus not on who "got it right," but on those comments that will assist them in sharpening their focus on the goal of the discussion.

Building three, four, or more participant comments or phrasings into your intervention provides acknowledging feedback without your posting endless evaluative comments that few people care to read. Drawing from both the tangential and the true, you encourage risk taking and foster a culture where participants are respected, even if they turn out to be "wrong."

Highlight tensions in the dialogue. Another strategy you can implement as the "Guide on the Side" is to seek tensions among comments. These are opportunities for you to encourage participants to clarify their reasoning, explore their underlying assumptions, and deepen the dialogue to levels of compelling interest for many.

Training Participants in a New Skill

In some online dialogue, direct feedback is part of the conversation. While fostering a culture of colearners, as the facilitator you can model the way participants might respond to their peers' work. At the same time, you should do everything to encourage participants to seek feedback from their peers and to offer it themselves. The course culture is most successful when participants offer constructive comments on each other's material without any outright encouragement per se.

In the two examples below, a TLC facilitator comments on draft outlines submitted by two students. The outlines are rough proposals for the secondary-level netcourses that each participant is developing. The facilitator's comments are in italic. She responded in depth to each participant's outline, asking clarifying questions, giving positive encouragement, including some humor, and offering technical and administrative advice.

Example 1

Assignment: Post the First One-Third of Your Course Outline in Week 4

This is a good start. I need to see more information about what are the main content and goals of each week. Like "the most important thing you will learn this week is how to... ." Also, adding URLs you have already found to each week would be useful. Have you seen the Monterey Bay Aquarium Web site?

[Moderator]

I. Start Here

    A. Welcome

    B. Expectations

        1. Assignments and Dates

        2. Work Quality

        3. Assessment

        4. Behavior

        5. Communication - Activity: Post your academic interests and the reason you chose to take this course.

May need to add LS orientation in Start Here; you can borrow material from TLC. There is a standard set of instructions we give to VHS students.

II. Week I: Introductions

    A. Teacher Introduction

    B. Student Introductions — Activity: Students will develop profiles.

    C. Getting Acquainted — Activity: Students will read profiles and post discussion on three classmates.

III. Week II: Introduction to Ocean Ecosystems

    A. Understanding Ecosystems — Activity: Read the article found in the MC. Post answers to the following questions:

    B. Marine Microbiology — Activity: Find and read two articles related to Marine Microbiology. Post a discussion summarizing your research.

Will students pick a research question and then do an investigation? Or will you provide a viewpoint/piece of evidence and have them critique whether to believe it or not? Say more about what research they will be doing.

    C. Communication — Activity: Compare your research to a classmate's. Post a discussion relating your research to that of your classmate.

IV. Week III: Productivity in Ocean Ecosystems

    A. Producers in Ocean Ecosystems — Activity: Students will read the article found in the MC. They will then discuss the various producers and their role in the Ecosystem.

V. Week IV: Abiotic Factors That Influence Ocean Ecosystems

    A. Activity: Students will research and identify the Abiotic factors that are part of Ocean Ecosystems. They will also read what their classmates have posted.

VI. Week V: Coral Reef Ecology

    A. Habitat — Activity: Describe the habitat for five organisms. Read what some of your classmates have posted and respond to two of them.

    B. Species — Activity: Students will research and report on three species found in the coral reef.

So far, there seems to be a lot of reading and posting in the course. How about a group activity or pairing students up? I'm no ocean expert, so you would have to figure out the content, but how about this? Have each student be an organism: You assign them one, but secretly via email or private thread; they describe their habitat to each other, what they like to eat, whether they like warm water, salt water, surge channels, etc. Then, each student has to guess what organism each student is. You might permit each student to ask another student two questions, like "Are you the size of a microbe?" or "Would a sea urchin like to eat you?"

Example 2

Feedback on Project SAIL

A good start. You had mentioned the use of "watch groups," logs, and lab experiments in your grading formula. I might make some explicit dates as to when you will check the journals and/or when you expect feedback from the watch groups. Also, since students are collecting their own vocabulary and terminology lists, were you planning to have students share this with others, or in pairs a couple of times during the semester in a "teach each other" kind of activity? One concern I have: Many of these activities look like they might actually be 2 weeks long, something to consider in the 15 weeks. Also, I didn't see any references to Titanic. Was this deliberate? :) Keep on revising and fleshing out details and wordings, and searching for good stuff.

PROJECT SAIL (altogether, 15 weeks is about right)

Week 1

Introduction to course

Complete personal profile

List 3 things that you hope to learn during this course

Pretest Survey

Week 2

View movie

? — Is this a digital movie, or something they can rent locally from the video store, or something you will mail to students? If you plan to mail materials, you send things to the local site coordinator, who will then distribute them to students.

Record terms, etc., not understood

Begin personal sailing glossary

Film survey — What two things did you like the most?

What two things were most confusing?

etc.

As participants learn a new skill — in this case, a new netcourse delivery system — direct feedback is the most constructive type of instruction. Here, in a goal-oriented course, it's not only desirable but imperative to "give answers" and positive reinforcement. Of course, you should temper this with a healthy dose of questions, where appropriate, to probe for deeper learning. The key is that you, the facilitator, not only offer such feedback, as in the examples above, but that the course design also encourages (even requires!) participants to do the same for one another. You maintain your stance on the sidelines, and the load on you thus remains manageable.

It's as hard as it is important to encourage both facilitators and participants to actually offer constructive feedback. People are shy, they don't want to be presumptuous, or they worry that they don't actually know what to suggest. In fact, from the recipient's point of view, comments are most appreciated — and as suggestions they remain optional. If members of a virtual community can be convinced of the safety of providing and receiving feedback, our experience is that everyone benefits from the collaboration.

Pyramid Model

We have found that once excellent course content and design are in place and a cadre of moderators are trained, a netcourse can be scaled up to reach more participants easily. Such an approach takes better advantage of the Internet as a medium, given the accessibility of web-based materials. In INTEC, seventeen moderators facilitated twenty cohorts of approximately twenty-five participants each, with one academic director overseeing the work of everyone (see Figure 3.3). During the second round, a group of our trained moderators could easily oversee additional cohorts moderated by the "rookie" moderators. These mentor moderators coach and oversee, while the academic director maintains overall quality and focus by supporting the mentors' work with the "rookies" who are working directly with participants alongside content-area Field Experts.

Sometimes it's easier to capture a vision by describing what it is not. We aren't suggesting here that even more proliferation of web junk be encouraged, or that netcourses be created and offered as quickly as possible and be taught to as many people as possible by as many "moderators" as can be dragged in off the street. We're thinking instead that if there are a few people with extraordinary expertise, the web makes it more possible to extend the traditional face-to-face reach of that expertise. Taking a netcourse is more interactive than simply reading an expert's book or working with his or her materials. If the design of the online workshop or course is done with input from that same expert, and others who know the work well (or the expert) are paired with a moderator trained in how to focus and deepen dialogue for enriched

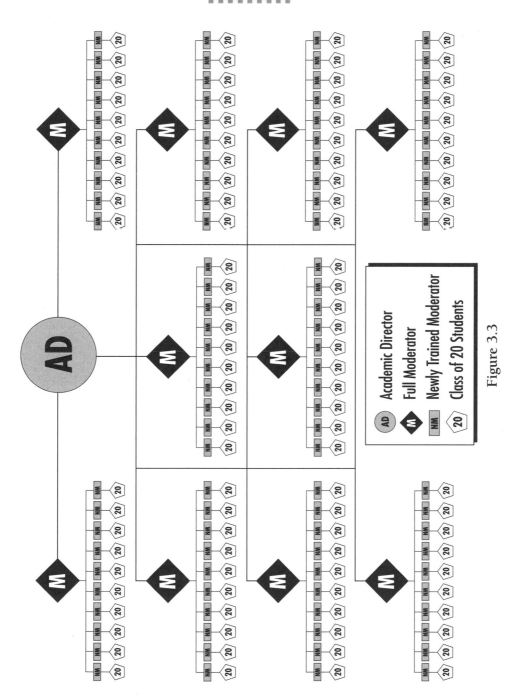

Figure 3.3

Legend:
- AD — Academic Director
- M — Full Moderator
- NM — Newly Trained Moderator
- 20 — Class of 20 Students

learning experiences, we could take much more advantage of the World Wide Web than is currently being done.

Scale is the temptation of the Internet, and clearly it can be a misused tool. Even people with a "name" or an association with a famous university could create a netcourse that wouldn't be an experience of the quality one would get studying with that person face to face. This is especially likely if the person has no training in online teaching beyond scanning famous lectures onto web pages. But with excellent netcourse design features and appropriate moderation, it is possible to scale quality — where there is quality worthy of scaling up, via something like the pyramid model we suggest here.

THE FACILITATOR AS INSTRUCTOR OR PROJECT LEADER

A misguided idea too often voiced in the context of netcourses is that using the network to deliver course content will replace teachers. There is no "teacher-proof" technology that can replace the careful attention and educational guidance provided by an experienced teacher. The network removes geographical constraints on interaction, but it does not change the instructor's central importance in learning. Student-teacher ratios will probably not change as we move to netcourses, but there may be many more teachers as well as students.

Whether or not you the facilitator of an online course are also the course designer or original teacher, you serve in an instructive role. However, if you're also a content expert, you'll greatly enhance course delivery and instruction if you become skilled at moderating. On the other hand, you may never need to become a content expert to be a good facilitator. For instance, as in INTEC, there may be a cofacilitator who visits your course only occasionally to serve as a content expert. Or perhaps your course will rely upon Internet-based "Ask A_____" (fill in the blank) services for expert answers and advice.

So what instructive role do all facilitators share? They can deepen the discussion and maintain a forward movement in the dialogue, thereby enriching the learning of the participants with respect to the subject of the collaboration.

Designing a Regular, Manageable Feedback Loop
In most courses, your role as facilitator will include developing a regular,

manageable feedback loop above and beyond the responses from you and your peers to the postings in the course discussion areas. Routine, private feedback between you and the netcourse participants promotes ease of communication with respect to any performance issues that arise. In a graded course, this is an essential part of keeping participants from feeling isolated and frustrated.

In the TLC — a graded course that teachers must pass to offer a course themselves in the Virtual High School — the feedback loop for each participant is in the form of a private, locked discussion thread. Only the individual participant and the instructor can access this private thread. It acts as "fast-track feedback," enabling the facilitator and the student to bring important information straight to each other's attention. The participant can use this thread to post any concerns, questions, or thoughts directly to the facilitator. The facilitator uses the thread to address private concerns and to post progress documents, comments, and grades for the student.

In the following post, the facilitator introduces herself to a new student and explains the purpose of the student's private thread. She tells the student that he shouldn't hesitate to use this discussion space to send her any questions or feedback throughout the course:

> Hi there,
>
> I am your contact person, helper, listener, and problem solver in this course. If you have any questions or concerns, please post something here in this space. I will be checking here first. If you need an answer right away, please send me email.
>
> I admit that I won't be able to answer the nitty-gritty details of LS the way Alice can, but think of me as a "learning partner": Two heads (and hearts) are better than one. If you have something to vent or any worries, please share with me.
>
> I hope things are going well in the course. Please do not hesitate to contact me for anything.

In addition to the individual discussion threads, the TLC also has general feedback discussion threads, open to anyone, that last for one week each. In these threads, students can publicly discuss any observations, questions, or concerns that have emerged from the week's lessons. The students take turns moderating these threads. Additionally, the TLC has several ongoing and very specific discussion threads facilitated by technical and content experts, where students can post very specific questions that can be shared with the entire class.

Separating content from process. Technical issues and questions about assignments — or *process*-related queries — are especially time sensitive. As facilitator, you need to respond to these questions as quickly as possible. In a netcourse in which all interactions and work submissions take place online and at a distance, participants may not be able to progress at all until they hear back from you. When participants are stuck in this way, they can start feeling isolated and frustrated at having to wait a long time for a response that will get them back on track.

Treat these process issues separately from course content by creating for each a specific discussion thread or main topic in the dialogue area. Then be consistent in using these threads, rather than other content-related dialogue areas or email, to respond to process issues. That way, your students won't confuse your moderating of content with the asking and answering of process questions — plus, your email will be greatly reduced!

Peer support. Earlier, we explained that online correspondence may quickly become overwhelming if you find yourself at the center of twenty individual conversations. For this reason, and because we think it's a better teaching model, our netcourses are designed so that the facilitator is on the side, directing and guiding multiple discussions that are taking place among the students. As students become more familiar with the online environment, the facilitator encourages them to share in the role of moderation. One of the important benefits of this approach is that over time, participants become more comfortable posting responses and questions to their peers, so that the facilitator doesn't need to post an individual reply to many questions posed in the discussion area. Some participants jump at opportunities to chime in and be helpful, confirming their own knowledge in the process. When it begins to happen in dialogues you facilitate, you know you've done something right!

It's important for you to not only establish avenues for regular feedback, but also to create an environment that welcomes student feedback on many levels. The following conversation between a facilitator and her students demonstrates this kind of feedback-friendly environment. The participants welcomed the chance to talk honestly with the facilitator about how the course was going, and most expressed gratitude that she was listening and responding to their input. This one posting from the facilitator sparked a discussion about the course that included fourteen postings total. Included here are two representative postings from that discussion:

Are the TLC Workload and Schedule Reasonable?

Comment to: Questions about the Course

[My co-facilitator] and I have been observing the rise and fall (and rise!) of participation in TLC. It would greatly help us if we knew what your preferences and habits were, and we could find out what is a reasonable level of participation. I understand that many of you do not have computer access on weekends. (I picture [a participant is named] running her dogs in the tundra of Alaska.) Our expectation is about five hours per week of interaction. Is this about right?

How often do you typically log in? Every other day? After school? Only on Fridays? Do you make a comment every time you log in or sometimes just read?

What do you think of the Wednesday through Tuesday schedule week? Does it make it harder or easier to complete assignments?

Thanks for your feedback. Holdin' my ear to the ground.

In this example, the facilitator senses that participants may have issues with the course that they are not adequately expressing to her. Thus, she specifically asks them for honest feedback about the course and whether or not they are feeling overwhelmed, so that she can best modify the course to encourage active participation.

Course Expectations

**Comment to: Are the TLC
Workload and Schedule Reasonable?**

I have a computer in my classroom and
some weeks I have spent 6 or 7 hours
and some only 2 or 3, depending on the
assignments and whether I can keep the
JAVA errors from shutting me down.
One thing I think that helps me is we are
on the block schedule, so I have a plan
every day of 1 and 1/2 hours, and if I get
a class going sometimes I can jump on
the Internet and answer questions and
do this at the same time. Most times I
enter something every time I get into the
class, and most of the time I do the work
on Tues., Wed., and Thurs. The Wed. to
Tues. schedule works fine, just because I
don't have access to the computer over
the weekend so I can finish on Mon. if I
need to.

I am enjoying learning all this, and
getting to listen to others' concerns helps
me. I appreciate all the hard work all of
you have put into on this course.

TLC and the "Real" World

**Comment to: Are the TLC
Workload and Schedule Reasonable?**

Well, I log on every day about the same
time to check my email and to do my
correspondence with my online bud-
dies. So when I do that, I've made it a
habit to come into TLC and check out
who's been here during the day. I'm
beginning to sort out who is who and
what kinds of personalities each of us are
bringing to this endeavor. I think that
once we got pedagogy out of the way

*Here's one participant's social response to
the moderator's social query.*

and we began to talk to one another, we started to relax a little with the course. I think that the week to catch up was helpful. The proposed schedule adjustment would be terrific so I won't have to choose between TLC and grading my essays. By the way ... the end of first semester is coming up for me, and I may be lost in grade land for a few days, so don't worry about me if I don't show up the week of the 20th. Thanks for the input request ... .

[Participant]

This social response offers a useful window into the participant's view of the course — telling the moderator (and colleagues) how the experience is "feeling" out there in the virtual classroom. Still new to the environment, this person's sense of the space and its potential is incomplete. The "letter-writing" style is a common approach to finding one's online voice.

THE FACILITATOR AS LEADER OF GROUP PROCESS

Your training and skill in moderating the group as a whole are critical for a successful collaboration. An online community exists only if its members are active and posting. A shy participant simply is not visible to the community if he or she doesn't join the discussion by posting messages in the discussion area. As the facilitator, you must draw all participants in and guide and focus the class discussions along constructive paths to learning. You must also pose questions and give reflective comments to help lead the students into deeper inquiry.

In order to ensure the success of the two facilitator roles we've already described — guide and instructor — there are some important group facilitation tasks you must either take on or appropriately delegate:

- Leading introductory, community-building activities
- Providing virtual "hand holding" to the digitally challenged
- Acknowledging the diversity of participants' backgrounds and interests
- Infusing personality with tone, graphics, and humor
- Maintaining a nurturing pace of responding
- Keeping up with the pace set
- Organizing posts and discussion threads
- Balancing private email and public discussion

Leading Introductory, Community-Building Activities

When you're about to begin a "regular" new course or workshop, the way you dress, fix your hair (or don't!), and choose your other visible accouterments — computer, briefcase, shoes — all contribute to the visual first impression participants get when they enter the door. In a virtual space, however, first impressions are built on text. Your introductory post is the participant's first window into who you are. Thus, you may find the task of writing this profile a challenge!

"Should I be witty? Should I list all of the awards I've received in the last five years? Should I just say it straight (deadpan), or should I insert some meta-commentary to 'spiff it up' and invite equally off-the-cuff chitchat from participants? Should I tell them about _____ (fill in the blank) or will that be too intimidating? Too boring? Too silly? Should I say I have three kids or should I leave it out? What about the dog? The dog stays in, right?"

Getting the presentational balance you want may take some thought and revision. This is a moment when our moderators are glad to have a peer group of colleagues with whom they can exchange personal profiles in order to get a better sense of the voice that feels "right" to them.

The second challenge is to then sit back and watch social community building occur among the participants, noting quotable phrases that will be useful for meeting the next challenge: focusing the group on the content ahead. The most successful moderator postings — right from the beginning — cite phrases and comments from the new participants that will then illuminate the path toward future focus and direction.

Another tact for inspiring participation and community shows up in the following excerpt from a moderator's post, in which he shares with his group his interaction with the "bag of goodies" all participants recently received in the mail:

> Last Thursday, on my way to class after lunch, I bumped into the UPS person delivering our EnviroChem box of goodies. I was like a kid at Christmas. I couldn't wait to open it. I was not disappointed, finding many new and exciting things for my students to do. The focus on nitrates seems logical to me, since we all have them in our environments. The range of experi-

ments and activities was welcome, since I have a diverse group of students. Now all I have to do is implement them with my students. The first thing I noticed was all the information about the twenty-eight schools in this strand. Although we do not have a CD-ROM at our school, we made arrangements to borrow one to show the kids and their parents the Almanac. At the same time, I designated three students to take on the task of rewriting a hello message from Central. Using the guide provided with seven areas to discuss, we will have a much more interesting hello message for the next CD-ROM. I thought schools like Inuksuk and School #345 had the most interesting messages from last fall. I wanted Central to reciprocate with a really interesting hello this time.

We have found that if the netcourse is organized around a compelling formula and has a critical mass of participants, then even those who are new to the technology will jump in with enthusiasm. In the TLC, the participants have a task they must get done. Their VHS netcourse — the one they're learning to design in the TLC — will become part of their local teaching load in the upcoming fall. Helping one another under what feels to many like "crisis" conditions (fast-paced, just-in-time) comes naturally in the asynchronous context of the TLC.

In INTEC, teachers are most engaged when they're learning a new tool to try in their own classrooms. Where else can teachers have ongoing discussions with others who are trying the same new teaching practices? Having a Field Expert who has already used the tool with his or her students is additionally compelling. Over the years of offering INTEC, we've found that the course didn't really take off until we had a critical mass of participants in every course section — between twenty and forty teachers. A group of that size gives both the talkers and the lurkers enough to motivate themselves to at least actively read, if not contribute to, the dialogue. While lurkers can be frustrating to group facilitators, we've found many who have been busy with the course materials and well satisfied with the course content. (Often our discovery of such teachers has been accidental; another local teacher will comment admiringly, or the school principal will comment in an INTEC evaluation. If your course isn't required and doesn't have required guidelines for participation, it can be quite fruitful to seek ways to learn what's really happening "out there."

Often, the activity in the discussion areas is only part of the work being done as a result of the course.)

Providing Virtual "Hand Holding" to the Digitally Challenged

Virtual "hand holding" is a phrase that's been used more than once to describe a phenomenon you'll find familiar if you already teach or lead an online group. Participants in netcourses, even those who don't consider themselves new to the digital world, seem to lose their usual set of problem-solving strategies in the new environment. Perhaps the lowered capabilities are a result of fear — fear of breaking the computer by experimenting, or fear of some lesser disaster: losing an hour's work, for instance. The participants' responses to the newness they confront is likely paired with bad experiences linked to the dearth of technical assistance available "out there" when it has been promised, even guaranteed. (These are mere hypotheses we've developed to explain what happens to participants in cyberspace when something goes wrong.)

To put the phenomenon in perspective, consider this analogy: When new friends visit, do they know their way around your house? Of course not. They've never been there before. Do your visitors panic when they don't know which way to go to reach the bathroom? No. They simply get directions. Although learning a new web environment is not a lot different than learning a new physical location, netcourse participants face the challenge somewhat differently. We find, for instance, that even when instructions are provided, some participants still need help interpreting the directions to the discussion area or a particular thread.

The dream of inventing a completely intuitive system of navigation is unlikely to be fulfilled, as course designs on the web abound. Instead, technical support — aka virtual hand holding — is essential in helping your "visitors" find their way. When so much of the web can be accessed so quickly (especially on a 56K modem or, faster still, a T1 connection!), netcourse participants get frustrated quickly indeed. In INTEC, we don't ask our moderators or professor to handle these exchanges. Instead, the role falls to the Project Coordinator. She receives emails like this one:

> MY MODEM WAS DOWN AND I WAS USING MY COL-
> LEAGUE'S COMPUTER AND NOW I CAN'T GET INTO THE
> DISCUSSION AREA. WHAT SHOULD I DO?

Though email is text-only, this participant's frustration is obvious. An understanding ear and a fix for the access problem are welcome relief for the participant, who just wants to get the assignment done without messing around with the technology.

While proficiency on the web and being "technically literate" are required for participation in a virtual working group or netcourse, even those who have earned online master's degrees often need help navigating through new web space. Similarly, no matter how many homes one has visited, accumulated expertise won't necessarily be useful in finding yet another discreetly placed bathroom. That's why INTEC is designed around two types of main web pages:

- The *schedule page*, which has links to all assignments
- The *discussion area homepage*, where five hundred participants can each access their cohort's discussions

To successfully complete assignments, participants must toggle back and forth between the two areas. The schedule page holds the actual "to do list" (e.g., reading assignments and activities), while the discussion area contains participants' postings.

"Technical support" sometimes means guiding participants to a new understanding of the medium, providing them with a framework for their own mental map of the web site. Although the structure seems easy, questions abound for a number of reasons. For some participants, the Internet is new territory. Even to those who are already initiated to the web, a netcourse uses the medium differently. It requires careful reading and deliberate use of certain web pages, not the more customary "scan-and-click" of standard surfing. As course developers learn to take advantage of the multimedia aspect of the web, which opens new avenues for course content delivery, so too participants must learn a new way to navigate through the multiple layers of information. Because the web is not a linear, textbook type of setting, our strategies for designing or taking a course online must be flexible.

Another participant writes:

> Would you please check my username and password? I used byxdyn394 as my password. [Note: This is an original, randomly generated password that we ask participants to

edit immediately so that it's something more personally memorable. Obviously this user hadn't yet taken that step.] I cannot get in. We are having our first meeting on Wednesday, and I desperately need to be online.

The Project Coordinator's response includes the username and a new, easy-to-remember password, along with a technical tip: "This is the direct URL for your cohort's discussion area. Be sure to bookmark it on all the computers you use to access the INTEC netcourse."

A signature "smiley face" emoticon :-)   serves as a source of comfort, to let the recipient know that help is available and happily given.

Acknowledging the Diversity of Participants' Backgrounds and Interests

By knowing the participants, you the facilitator can better create a safe environment in which the participants feel comfortable taking risks and giving feedback. While creating a safe environment is important for any facilitator, it's especially critical in an online setting, where participants may more easily feel alienated or isolated from the community, or intimidated by the technology. Participants in a netcourse may also represent a more diverse range of backgrounds and experiences than participants in a face-to-face setting, as the flexibility of the netcourse setting allows people from around the world to study together.

In order to create a safe environment, then, you need to structure the course and its activities in a way that is open to participants' diversity and builds community among all. Finding ways to attend to all of the participants' backgrounds, ages, and geographical locations is essential. There are also technology differences to acknowledge: General experience, computer platform, and access to varying levels of "techie" accessories — animation tools, software, scanners, and such. Adding an online survey to the course registration or the introductory activities could help you gather such pertinent information.

Simple, structural details will reveal your attention to such issues. For example, keeping the netcourse asynchronous and moving it at a weekly (rather than daily) pace allows participants nationwide or even worldwide to participate according to their own schedules. Assigning due dates by day rather than by time (e.g., "This assignment is due Friday," rather than

"This assignment is due Friday at 5:00 p.m. sharp") gives participants in different time zones equal footing. (In the first year of VHS, West Coast high school students in the U.S. felt that the 3:00 p.m. deadlines assigned by their East Coast teachers were unfair!) Also, if there is a time-sensitive event (like a first-come, first-served sign-up for something), you and any other group leaders should take into consideration that participants may be in different time zones; thus, you should adjust the event accordingly. (VHS student registration, for instance, is done on a first-come, first-served basis, but registration starts at 12:00 noon Eastern Standard Time to equalize the opportunity for the most registrants.)

Another way to acknowledge the participants' diversity is to discuss with them the option of sharing photos of themselves online. We have found that many netcourse participants appreciate the "fresh start" they get by being visually anonymous in an online setting. For many, this will be the first time they aren't concerned about their age, weight, dress, hair, any physical disabilities, etc., when contributing to class discussions. If personal photos are posted online, you might suggest that participants consider such alternative depictions as a drawing, a cartoon caricature, or a story or poem, leaving individuals' options open with respect to what they wish to post.

An effective way to approach the unevenness in participants' technical tools and savvy is to craft assignments and projects that can be done largely offline, with results and comments being posted online after the work is done. While any netcourse will have certain minimum technology-access requirements, there are ways to accommodate participants who have varied technical access and experience. For example, all TLC participants must use certain browser versions to interface successfully with the course delivery software. But the TLC is designed for either Mac or Windows access from any computer with an adequate Internet connection. Users need only the appropriate browser and their personal password to access the course anywhere, anytime. They can access it from home on a PC one day and from a Mac at their office the next. As facilitator, you're better off avoiding software that can be used only on a single platform. If a particular skill or type of experience isn't required to participate in the course, you should assume that some students are beginners. You can always "hide" detailed instructions behind a link for participants to skip or access, depending on their skill level.

Infusing Personality with Tone, Graphics, and Humor

Skill in setting tone and infusing personality and humor into netcourse discussions is essential for anyone seeking to facilitate online dialogue. One of the first challenges you must solve as moderator is that of how you put your own face forward — breaking the virtual ice — in a social or academic discussion area. The online community may know you solely by what you post online. Therefore, you should decide what type of tone you want to set in the self-introductory assignments. Do you want to post a formal photo? Or a self-drawn caricature? One facilitator posted a silly animated GIF to represent herself, lightening the intensive course material she was delivering. Another resisted the formal head-and-shoulders portrait of faculty handbooks and used an informal pose with his kid on vacation. (Note: Discussion areas permit attachments of GIF images.)

Participants respond in kind, or at their level of comfort. Some of the participants in INTEC and the TLC have introduced themselves through pictures with their horses; others have given descriptions of themselves; and still others have included photos of their summer cabins or fishing boats, or snapshots of their children and families, hobbies, or classrooms. These visual elements and the associated descriptions go a long way toward establishing a sense of the "classroom" and its virtual inhabitants.

The tone- and personality-setting task continues throughout the course. For example, you must consider how you wish to be addressed. With a nickname? A title? Does Dr. or Professor, within the context of the institution and the course, help the dialogue, or does a more informal approach yield better returns? Commonly, facilitators interject some sort of brief personal note or story into their posts; these descriptions serve as part of the ritual element of social dialogue cited earlier. Bits about insights you've had while driving to work, reactions you've had when talking to colleagues or family, or simple musings help the participants identify with you as the facilitator and feel comfortable sharing anything with you. Personal anecdotes may also help make the course and the content more accessible to participants who are intimidated by the new medium.

You can also gather important clues about the level of interaction with course content by looking for the social elements in participants' posts. You can then lend a hand as the participants move from facility with social dialogue to substantive interactions.

You can continue building a sense of shared space and community by paying attention to the personal experiences of assignments and the context of the course. In the following message, for instance, the moderator combines text and graphics to get the participants' attention as she urges them to complete their work. She also uses this example to offer a mini-lesson on how participants' can include graphics in their own postings:

A Word from Your Electronic Teacher …

Comment to: Questions about the Course

Hello class,

This is the last week that I get to lead the TLC. Before I sing my swan song, I need to do some electronic nagging. Next week, I anticipate a surge of stress, electronic glitches, cries for help, and lost passwords. It's the highway to installing LearningSpace!

Please PLEase PLEASE! Try to finish all of your late assignments from Weeks 1-12, and do your best to get 13 done. I know it's flu season and the wires are also sick, but keep your spirits up! You are pioneers! You can do it!

I recently found out that chocolate gives Carla headaches. So I am sharing some virtually fat-free dried fruit from near my hometown in Silicon Valley, California, from when it used to be known for its 12" topsoils and lovely orchards. Also, a PowerBar™ for an extra boost of energy to you all. Bon sante!

Oh, and by the way, it took me a couple of tries, but I figured out how to post this image inside this window instead of as an attachment (which saves hard disk space and doesn't risk copy-right issues). Just type square brackets around this HTML tag.

<IMG SRC= "http://www.primo.com/clients/su_marip.jpg">

Graphics in support of environment and learning. Graphics, particularly those of a gratuitous or figurative variety, can be a considerable annoyance to participants who are accessing a course through a low-bandwidth connection. Graphic elements, however, can greatly increase a participant's feeling of support and personal attention if they're seen as aids or hints to overcoming misunderstandings of graphical interfaces or accessing information in system or program requirements. With a technique that feels like a "Tutor over One's Shoulder," TLC and INTEC facilitators and instructors often use "screen shots" — images of windows, menus, or screens as they appear on a user's computer — to illustrate by example. The following screen shot is one an instructor might use to discuss computer basics:

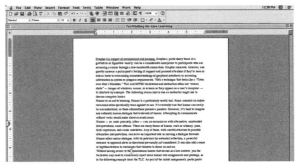

Screen shot reprinted by permission from Microsoft Corporation

Humor as an aid to learning. Humor is a particularly useful tool. Some manuals on online communication specifically warn against its use. It's certainly true that humor can easily be misunderstood, so these admonitions present a paradox. However, it's hard to imagine any authentic human dialogue that is devoid of humor. Attempting to communicate without verbs would make about as much sense.

Humor — or, more precisely, jokes — can, on occasion or with alternative, unintended interpretations, cause offense. There are many forms of humor, such as whimsy, puns, droll expression, and comic anecdotes. Any of these, with careful attention to possible alternative interpretations, can serve an important role in moving a dialogue forward. Humor offers online dialogue, with its potential for extended reflection, a powerful resource to approach ideas in directions previously not considered. It can also add a sense of lightheartedness to exchanges that threaten to drone on and on.

Without having access to the spontaneous humor that occurs in a live context, you the facilitator may need to consciously inject some humor into assignments and postings, as in the following example from the TLC. As part of the initial assignments, participants take a "virtual field trip" to the courses designed by several previous TLCers. The assignment offers a whimsical tour of potential practice for newcomers to the TLC, and provides a rich set of experiences as well as a wonderful basis for dialogue.

VHS Field Trip, Course Outlines, and Overview

Did everyone bring their Internet driver's license and a bag lunch? This week we will walk the virtual halls of the Virtual High School. First, we will view some pristine "demo" courses — courses that have all student work removed. Then, later on in the week, we will visit two live courses, complete with students! Several teachers have granted us permission to visit their courses, but we must follow the field trip rules:

1. Under no circumstances will we make any written comments in these courses, and
2. we will not interact or correspond with any students during or after the trip.

We will have an opportunity to ask questions of the pioneering VHS teachers later on.

After these visits, you will be creating the first draft of your netcourse as an outline.

OK! Let's go take a look at a few demo courses.

Informal Geometry: A Construction Approach

Writing, from Inner Space to Cyberspace

To introduce this assignment, the facilitator creates a humorous graphic depicting herself and some of the other faculty members in a "virtual school bus" heading off on a field trip together. In fact, the assignment really is the equivalent of going on a virtual field trip; the students actually visit VHS courses taught by previous TLC graduates to see successful examples before they start creating their own netcourses. The facilitator counters her serious lecture on "rules" by placing it in the humorous context of a field trip. Everyone remembers mandatory "field trip rules" lectures from their school days. The sense of excitement among the TLC participants was palpable in the posts both before and after the trip.

This handmade graphic with its inside joke fosters — maybe more so than a seriously stated, text-based assignment would — a sense of community, and helps participants feel like they're off on an exciting learning adventure together. Of course, the facilitator will probably find that as the online community becomes closer, participants will begin to express their senses of humor spontaneously via cartoons, pictures, and words — just as they would in a face-to-face community.

Serious students of humor inform us that humor relies on a simultaneous juxtaposition of two levels of interpretation; one common, another unusual. Groucho Marx's famous line — "Last night I shot an elephant in my pajamas. What he was doing there I'll never know." — is a timeless example. The discord between the two interpretations jolts the mind from one view to another. The resulting disconnect can serve the purpose of providing entertainment, as in the example above; or instruction, in which a mind or group of minds may seem caught in a rut before the multiple perspectives supplied by humor provide a way out of fixated thought.

In the following example from INTEC, the facilitator invites secondary algebra teachers to alternatively interpret some work with math manipulatives. Some had viewed the manipulatives as elementary school toys. Others had grappled with the expression of squares or cubes of numbers as real arrangements of objects (snap-together cubes). Three cubed, for example, was viewed as a cube of twenty-seven units, three units on a side.

MESSAGE SUBJECT: Evidence of Early Algebra Found

In a cave high in the French Pyrenees, a startling discovery was made.

Did any of the work we did with surface area blocks or "Visualizing Algebra" bring new insights on algebra? Or was it older than the rocks?

In this activity, participants work with connectable cubes and explore what squares and cubes look like. They are challenged to see what algebraic expressions like $(X + 1)^2$ or $(X + 1)^3$ would look like.

In a response to this activity, one participant wrote:

I realized we were representing one of the most common formulas of Algebra 2: $(a+b)^3 = a^3 + 3a^2b + 3ab^2 + b^3$. **I had used this formula for 30 years**, because I was told to memorize it and was taught where to apply it, **but I never really understood what it meant.** This is very exciting and mind boggling to suddenly, after all these years, make a concrete representation of the formula.

Humor can also gently remind participants of the potential for misconceptions, even when a communication might seem completely clear to the author. This added layer of meaning — seeing from the learner's perspective and checking assumptions — can promote a deeper level of dialogue. In the example below from INTEC, a moderator uses a graphic in this way:

The assignment asks, "Where did this inquiry with manipulatives and algebra teaching go?"

A teacher can honestly ask, "Do I want my class to go there? How does it fit with my curriculum?"

More HARD QUESTIONS follow quickly.

Even if I did try these tools out, as an algebra teacher I can wonder, "What use are the manipulatives, and how do they help with abstract thinking?"

The assignment asks us to consider, How does one make the transition to symbolic thinking? Is there a pedagogical gain?

[Moderator]

Humor is one tool, among many others. If you have a humorous bent, be careful to balance your approach for those who don't appreciate the lighter side of dialogue. The caveat is to use what you feel will work with your group while at the same time keeping it interesting and in service of advancing the dialogue.

Maintaining a Nurturing Pace of Responding

Logistically, as facilitator you probably won't be able to respond individually to every post. This presents a dilemma — especially if you're a seasoned classroom teacher or trainer accustomed to the face-to-face venue, where you can slip in at least a silent acknowledgment of participants' contributions without interrupting the flow of conversation. While private email might be the parallel to a silent nod in an online dialogue, it is equally untenable as a way of acknowledging your virtual participants.

In an inquiry-based course, you encourage students to respond to each other's messages, so that they learn to rely less on individual feedback from you for every question and thought. This is certainly how community-building activities tend to go naturally. But once a course is in gear and the introductions are over, the dialogue moves to content-based commentary. The goal here is to keep the cross commentary going where it naturally subsides in a live venue, as participants sit back, relax, and start listening (daydreaming?) after the socializing is over and class is starting. In an online discussion, you must decide how to respond in a way that keeps participant involvement high. One strategy is to sit on your proverbial "virtual hands" when a dialogue begins, jumping in only after participants have posted some (seven or eight?) comments.

How long to wait is a function of both how many participants post right away and how much time is going by. It calls for a bit of intuition about the complexity of the assignment, the unusually heavy scheduling issues participants might be facing at that moment, and other, similar considerations. (It's not unlike deciding when to unplug the popcorn popper when, in the last few seconds before pulling the plug, you might think, "Is there more? Is it done? More silence … time to act.") Then you can post a comment highlighting the most salient comments, putting them together to focus on their common theme or their inherent tensions or their potential for further dialogue; thus, you set a new context or frame. (In Chapters 5 and 6, respectively, we address in detail the voice and tone you can use for such a post, and exactly what to do with the excerpted dialogue elements in your intervention.) Such inquiry-based synthesis pushes participants to think further about the issues raised. At the same time, it acknowledges the most valuable contributions to the dialogue — without your having to respond individually to each one.

To deepen a discussion, it's important to emphasize only the most constructive contributions made by the participants. It's also essential, however, for you to respond to all participants equally in quality and volume. The only interaction a participant has with you is in the form of posts, and so a participant can feel quite vulnerable if multiple posts go unanswered or aren't cited by you (or the rest of the community). Software like Lotus Notes' LearningSpace™ has an Assessments/Portfolio module that allows you to easily keep track of the postings and assignments submitted by each of your students. If you aren't using such software, setting up a standardized progress record for each student will help keep you (as well as each student) organized and aware of both whom you've received input from and whom you've responded to with feedback.

Of course, technical questions need immediate response to keep participants engaged and feeling productive and capable. Maintaining an ongoing, separate discussion thread for technical questions, and fostering its consistent and appropriate use, works well.

Deciding when to respond. As facilitator, you must continuously judge the appropriate pace of responding to participants' posts. Which posts are time-sensitive or require quick turnaround? When is it more sensible to remain quiet and let the participants take over? You're faced with a unique situation in the netcourse setting: All interactions are asynchronous and at a distance. If you're an uninitiated virtual facilitator, it can be difficult to know how to appropriately direct an unfolding discussion. Along with getting a sense of the pace that feels right, carefully considering a rationale for intervening is critical to maintaining your position on the sidelines.

Silence, on the other hand, can be equally stifling, as participants may interpret a slower pace of response on your part as intentional for some reason. They may start to think that you're offended by or disappointed with the posting(s), or that you haven't been online and therefore you must not care. Early on, while a culture of friendly feedback is being fostered, you may want to email participants about their new postings or technical achievements as a way of balancing encouragement to active participants with leaving space for others to respond publicly in the discussion areas. If participants' first efforts are greeted with silence, especially if they've gone out on a limb and tried something brand new, they may be more hesitant to take risks next time. Or, if they think no one is reading their contributions, they may become discouraged from posting further.

When you successfully encourage a culture of colearners, participants will readily comment on one another's postings, relieving you of sole responsibility.

Synthesizing and refocusing a waning dialogue. A netcourse often demands more disciplined time management and independent motivation from participants than a traditional face-to-face course would. Our netcourses are designed on a weekly time frame to accommodate national and international schedules. This setup, coupled with the fact that teachers are never physically present with the students, can have the unfortunate side effect of increased procrastination on the part of the students, which subsequently leads to lagging discussions. Here's a good example of what you might post to stimulate a faltering discussion:

Hi all,

I just wanted to let you all know that [my co-facilitator] and I are hanging here in the wings waiting to help answer any questions you might have about pedagogical aspects of designing a netcourse, or concerns you might have about teaching in the virtual environment and how to make it more effective.

Would you like private/public feedback on your netcourse so far? We have access to everyone's course and can view your work. Just give us a holler.

The facilitator uses this post to remind the group that she's available to help, and that she's monitoring the participants' progress (or lack thereof). She also uses the post to give the group a gentle nudge, reminding them of the course posting expectations.

Also, I'm aware of the tight schedule of schools that are finishing at the end of May, and that spring fever has hit. Turns out my stand partner in the Los Alamos Symphony is a sophomore in high school just dying for summer to come early and to see pictures from the prom. Another violinist is a math teacher who gave out a take-home exam and only received a disappointing 50% return.

Hope all is well with you. Don't forget to check into the TLC at least once a week to let us know you're alive and kicking.

The facilitator keeps the reminder friendly and accessible by including a personal story, and by acknowledging that this is a busy time of year for those in education.

Keeping Up with the Pace That's Been Set

If your course is active, you the facilitator are presented with the additional challenge of keeping up once a healthy pace has been set. Even without many side email conversations to curb or contend with, keeping up with the discussions and completed assignments can challenge even the most organized leader! Nevertheless, keeping up is essential, lest the group lose its progress.

Some moderators we know print everything posted to their course and put the paper into individual student folders, so that they have something tangible to assess. Hopefully, this is only a transitional stage in moving from the physical to the virtual classroom! However, a paper gradebook or spreadsheet may be useful in helping you assess the progress of virtual students, simply because the process may mean having a number of windows open in your course simultaneously to do the work. The technologies being used and your personal preferences will determine what combination of paper and online information processing works best for you. A system of tracking participants' work that makes the most sense to you is better than any general "formula."

One tool that any new facilitator may find useful is a communications plan. Such a plan might be as simple as following a prescribed routine after logging in: Checking current group discussions first for new posts; looking at private discussion threads (individual student threads), then at the "Tech" thread and the "Questions about Assignments" thread; and, finally, checking emails. Your communications strategy might also include contingency plans for perceived inactivity: When overall participation is low, you could send a group email like the one just cited; When specific individuals are inactive, private emails might help you identify individual problems participants are having with course access or time management. In extreme cases, even phone calls are a good idea.

Organizing Posts and Discussion Threads

There are several organizational techniques for posting assignments and discussion threads that are useful for you to foster as the facilitator of an online community. A threaded discussion and the database software that supports it can be confusing and counterintuitive to the novice. Just convincing new users not to apply an "email" mindset to the experience is an important step toward taking advantage of the threaded nature of a discussion area.

Often, people who are new to netcourses voice frustration that course commentary isn't coming directly to their email inbox, as listserv messages do. However, the randomness of listserv activity can't lend itself to the depth of discussion and potential for insight and learning that a threaded set of posts ordered in an outline format can. Once people learn to visit their discussion areas as automatically as they open their email, complaints about separate discussion areas disappear.

Once acclimated, participants often make such common mistakes as creating new main discussion threads when they should have responded to existing ones, or submitting new messages without clear subject headings. Regarding the placement of participants' posts, you should provide clear instructions on where to post. Participants often put questions about any subject that's on their mind inside whatever posting they happen to be crafting — a phenomenon that quickly creates a disorganized online discussion area. Questions should, of course, be encouraged, but there should be distinct areas for them. It's much easier for everyone if questions on assignments are kept separate from, for example, questions on technology. How can you do this? By simply starting two main threads with these general titles and directing participants to use them.

To encourage good use of threaded text at an early stage, you might lead by example, as the facilitator did in the following "posting about posting" found in the TLC:

Questions about the Course

Comment to: Virtual Office Hours

Hi,

Please use this discussion thread for questions and discussion about the TLC. This "whiteboard" thread is for comments about the readings, concerns about the TLC pace, and other course issues.

[One of the moderators] has created two additional topic threads for "Questions about Assignments": There's one thread for questions about how to complete assignments, and there's a second for asking technical questions.

See the first topic posted below; this as an example of an appropriate thread for what we've dubbed the "whiteboard."

The facilitator offers specific instructions on how and where participants should post certain questions. Then she tells them where to look for a concrete example.

As facilitator, you might set an even better example by actually relocating a post that was submitted in the improper thread:

Hi everyone!

I've lifted three great, related postings from the CourseRoom today and pasted the thread below. Why would I do such a thing to good info, you ask? It's because I'm the obsessive-compulsive type who likes an extremely organized CourseRoom. Pat asked a good question, and Susan quickly gave her a helpful answer, but it all took place in a separate discussion, away from the "Questions on Assignments" discussion topic we set up for this kind of question.

The facilitator moved these postings because they were in an inappropriate thread. Note that her tone adds humor and builds on a social element. Rapidly she moves to the main point — a needed clean-up. She humors contributors but firmly directs participants to proper posting protocols.

I hope Pat and Susan will forgive me for publicly announcing the redoing of their documents, but I have to actually copy and paste the text into a new document and can't just move them quietly. LearningSpace doesn't provide the feature of simply recategorizing documents into another existing topic.

Moving a person's post could make that person feel singled out. To ensure this doesn't happen, the facilitator makes an example of a "great" post and makes sure to state that she's moving it mostly because she wants to be able to share it with the entire class.

When you begin teaching your own courses, you'll be faced with this same situation. Your choices will be to: Redo

By moving a posting early on in the course, the facilitator teaches with a concrete visual example. Such modeling can serve to counter the confusion that many participants may feel about where and how to post.

the documents yourself (which is nice at the beginning, while your students are still learning how this crazy thing all works); have your students redo their submissions where you want them (which is nice later into the course); or leave the submissions wherever they land (which can get quite chaotic over time).

So, here they are …

Message subjects. A common problem in threaded discussions is that people reply to a main thread without paying attention to subject title. For example, under a general thread called "Activity One Discussion," there may be a long list of replies, all labeled "Re: Activity One Discussion," if participants neglect to change the message subject or thread title. Your (or your colleagues') search, then, for a particular comment (e.g., "Where was that interesting comment I just read about using probes in the classroom?") becomes all too often a lengthy hunt among threads that have little to differentiate them.

You can model thread naming in a way that spurs discussion by honoring the contributions of participants. Using phrases coined in the discussion area as message subjects attracts the attention of at least the original contributor. For example, "This is driving me nuts" was one thread title, and a participant quote, in one of the INTEC discussion areas. It surely got some notice! Another strategy is to actually put people's names on the message subject. Catching a participant's attention directly with his or her name can help convey the idea that it is his or her ideas you're acknowledging.

Metaphors, paradoxes, and humorous language also encourage and pull the group together. Titles that are eye catching, while serving to frame the content of the posts, engage the participants in the conversation. Consider these actual message subject titles, taken from the INTEC course:

- "Midwifing a Dragon's Delivery"
- "The Pesky Kreb's Cycle"

- "Does Thinking Stop at the Edge of a Model?"
- "Balancing Acts"
- "Keep on Truckin'"
- "The Kids Were 'Talking about Math,' and Other Tales of Successes"
- "Looking Back to Move Ahead"
- "Great Idea? Or Moment of Weakness?"

Optimizing the use of threaded discussion areas. Even when there have been significant postings, a common problem that can arise is that many posts are one-shot efforts posted directly to the main thread. Often, it seems participants will view their contributions as notes sent to the teacher or leader, not as comments woven into a dialogue. Despite the initial community-building efforts within the group, these participants continue to see themselves as individuals, not as collaborators in a larger effort; email remains the mindset.

As facilitator, you must be ready to build bridges to a better understanding of the opportunities inherent in the threaded format for deepened, focused discussion. There are at least two techniques you can try in your attempts to do this. One is to craft a comment that cites a number of participants, and then post it as a reply to one of the most interesting postings in the dialogue. Your citations should be from the "loner" posts so that you can bring them into the main dialogue. It's also wise to include a link to the post you are citing ...

[<A HREF="url to full posting"TARGET=NEW> Mary says</A>]

... and then include a pithy excerpt. The link will take the reader to the full posting in a new browser window. Depending on the content of the clips, you might hold them up as key points in a discussion oriented toward a certain goal, or as differing views that may be pointing to a deeper commonality or truth. Through such a posting, you model a more threaded style of dialogue in the discussion area; at the same time, you focus the discussion and move it forward.

The second strategy is to name a "loner" in the message subject amidst an interwoven chunk of dialogue, and then do what we suggested above: Point to the common views held or the potential for further dialogue among the participants.

Balancing Private Email and Public Discussion

The TLC is set up so that as much of the course as possible takes place in one central area — the LearningSpace virtual classroom, which is open to all participants. Participants are encouraged to share their comments, discussions, questions, and work with each other and the instructor in the regularly accessed "CourseRoom" area. This is as much to maintain organization as it is to foster collaborative community. Participants are told that they should not send assignments or general discussion questions to the facilitator via email. They're encouraged instead to post most everything into the CourseRoom.

However, VHS also maintains several email listservs (i.e., distribution lists) for quickly broadcasting administrative information and announcements. Participants in an asynchronous netcourse may log into the course only several days in any given week, and they probably won't read every recent posting in any one sitting. Therefore, an informational listserv is an efficient and reliable way to assure that general information and announcements reach every participant on a timely basis.

In addition, as facilitator you may wish to create a prominent "bulletin board" space or welcome page within the netcourse itself, so that you can display important notices to all of your students. In the INTEC course, for example, a general notice at the top of each discussion area contains brief announcements or links to information for participants.

A moderating challenge that is unique to the online setting is finding the optimal balance between private email and public discussion. In a face-to-face setting, it's fairly easy to limit private and public discourse. A set number of office hours and the designated course meeting times create boundaries that are naturally enforced by the institutions that create them. New groups of students move into the room as classes end, other students are also in line to meet with the professor during office hours, buildings get locked, and so on.

Establishing such balance isn't as easy in an online setting, where all communication happens asynchronously. As facilitator, you can quickly become overwhelmed by too many labor-intensive, private email conversations in addition to the numerous postings in an active public discussion area. Also, participants who are eager for personalized contact with you may send you their assignments or work in a private email that would be more appropriately sent to their classmates in the online community. You can optimize your time and improve the quality of participants' discussions by encouraging the participants to post most of their questions and comments in the public discussion areas. (Of course, truly private issues should still be handled in personal emails.) Encouraging participants to comment on one another's work, instead of setting the expectation that all the feedback will come from one source — you — sets an important precedent in a culture of inquiry where you're not the only participant with valuable expertise.

Lotus Notes' "LearningSpace™" software also allows students to post private messages that can be locked and made accessible only to the instructor. Organizationally and administratively, it can be very useful for both the students and you the facilitator to have all interactions located in one area, so that there is a complete record of work done at all times. Private emails may be more easily overlooked or misplaced than private, locked postings located right in the CourseRoom with the other class postings.

There are, of course, occasions when a private email (or even a phone call) is more efficient and appropriate than any other method of communication. Personal issues may be best discussed in a private setting outside of the virtual CourseRoom (although, as we often see in the TLC, a strong community will offer an outpouring of support and consolation in response to members' personal problems). An interaction around a personal or sensitive issue can feel more meaningful one-on-one in an email or phone call than in a private posting.

Very specific administrative or technical questions, as well as congratulations to personal triumphs, might also be more appropriately discussed via email, so as not to clutter the CourseRoom. However, even if a technical or administrative exchange seems very specific, it might actually be useful to other members of the community. The three examples below clarify the distinctions we're making:

Example 1

[Moderator],

Thanks for talking me through my nervous breakdown. I like your analogy of Notes as a friend from another country ... with a different language and customs. (Men are from Mars, Women are from Venus, Lotus Notes is from Zoltron.) I am getting up my courage to do what you suggested, but just knowing there is a voice at the end of the phone line makes me feel better.

[A participant]

Here, a participant thanks one of the instructors in the public CourseRoom for being there for her one-on-one via phone at a time when she was really frustrated. The comment reveals sufficient comfort to post boldly.

Example 2

Hello — I see you have made two attachments already on February 6. I can see a paperclip icon to the left of the heading, so I know that there is an attachment. When I click on the link to the attachment at the bottom of the window, I can open the document in MS Word 6, although it is garbled at the top. (I assume you are using MS Word 7 and I don't have the right translator program.)

What further information do I need to send you, to get specific help?

Hi [Participant],

Send me email for a faster reply. In terms of standardizing on a word processor, that is up to the rest of the TLC staff. I use MS Word 6 on a Mac, which is cross-platform-compatible with a PC. I am going to Concord for a face-to-face meeting this Friday. Will let you all know the results.

[Moderator]

In this response to a participant's technical problems, the facilitator answers the main question in the public setting (so that others may learn from it as well), but also tells the participant that he should email her too, so that they can quickly address and resolve specific problems.

Example 3

Am I Getting It All?

I have so much trouble with my computer and my link-up that I think I have missed so much, and I have looked in assignments, and discussions, and schedule to find the work. How can I be sure I am doing all that I should?

Clarification on Assignments Comment to: Am I Getting It All?

Hi,

There are indeed a lot of assignments, and one can easily become over-whelmed. Hang in there! If you'd like to ask one of us specifically about how you are doing, feel free to send us electronic mail. Also, we have set up topics in the CourseRoom called "So-and-So's Prog-ress" (whoever is the student). Although this is posted in the Course-Room, only you and the instructors have access to this information. This is like a progress report card of the assignments you've completed.

If you are referring to Weeks 1-3, there are some self-assessments that you can take to see if you've mastered the assign-ments. They are designed to help you get around LearningSpace screens.

For Week 4, I am looking for a total of three comments made to discussion topics posted for Week 4. Please see the assignment posted under the Schedule database's blue twistie for Week 4. Hope this helps. If not, give us a virtual hoot.

[Moderator]

The facilitator senses from this participant's posting that she may be feeling over-whelmed, and that a private, one-on-one email may be the best way to make her feel better and address her concerns. She gives the participant the option of either sending a private email or posting a private document in the CourseRoom, but at the same time she tries to address the technical problem in this public setting.

In fact, other participants also may have this question. In this case, it's quite helpful for the facilitator to be able to clarify in this public setting the work students are expected to complete.

These strategies illustrate ways of improving the quality in, and smoothing the process of, a netcourse. Their consistent use contributes to the overall health and goal-oriented nature of the course and the work group environment.

In the next chapter, we explore how you can assess the culture of your course's collaborations and how you might improve it. Our experience suggests that the old adage, "If I teach just one person how to …" is no longer the standard you can feel satisfied to achieve. If the content is excellent and the moderating support effective, the limits of time and space need no longer keep superior teachers and excellent courses finite and localized. When excellent work is being done via online collaboration, the setting is a functional online group. And so we identify and describe, in Chapter 4, several criteria for evaluating virtual group health.

Chapter Four

HEALTHY ONLINE COMMUNITIES

■ FUNCTIONAL ONLINE GROUPS

A "healthy," web-based, collaborative learning community has the following characteristics:

- Participants post regularly.
- The online community meets its members' needs, and participants express honest opinions.
- Participant-to-participant collaboration and teaching are evident, and spontaneous moderating occurs among the participants.
- Reasonable venting about technology, content, and even the facilitator is acceptable and evident.
- Participants show concern and support for the community.

This chapter will give you our best insights on these criteria — though surely new criteria will be added to our list as experience with online teaching and virtual teamwork grows and matures.

Participants Post Regularly

This guideline is purposefully vague, and it takes on different meanings in various contexts.

In a product work group, the regularity of posting can be reflective of how open the lines of communication are among team members, managers, and the group leader. Participation may emerge in spurts of activity as problems develop and get resolved in the online dialogue. On the other hand, when work moves smoothly and deadlines are being met, there may be less need for dialogue.

In netcourses, an appropriate amount of posting may take on added meaning if there is an expectation of a required number of postings for credit or for a grade. Gauging the quality of postings and the interactions among participants then becomes, of course, a more critical task. As the instructor or group leader, you should check for appropriate use of the threaded nature of the dialogue as well as evidence of learning occurring in the comments participants offer.

To establish a healthy community from the start, TLC facilitators clearly define participant guidelines and expectations at the beginning of the course. In the TLC design, there are no face-to-face encounters, so the only way to assess a participant's progress is to read the discussions and assignments he or she has posted in the virtual classroom. When the only way to participate is to comment, there's no such thing as "sitting silently in the back of the room" and receiving credit for attending a meeting or class.

In the following TLC outline of guidelines for students, satisfactory course participation is defined not only in terms of quantity, but also in terms of the quality of discussion and assignment postings:

Guidelines for Posting:

Lessons are listed under the week titles in the schedule. These lessons have a due date assigned and should be completed in the order they are listed.

Since each week contains several activities, it is best to try to complete the activities throughout the work week and not leave all of them until the last day.

You're expected to participate fully in all assignments and complete them on time.

Ask for help or information early on if you don't understand something. Remember, you're responsible for getting what you need! We're here to help you.

You will be assessed mainly by your participation in the discussions. Many

While each online community will have its own minimum requirements for participation, a guidelines document like this one can help you emphasize from the beginning that posting in the course regularly is essential.

of the activities throughout the course will require you to either participate in a group discussion on a specific topic or to research something and post your thoughts.

Your postings should be thorough and thoughtful. Just posting an "I agree/disagree with your comment" or an "I think the same" to someone else's thoughts is not considered to be an adequate response. We will cover this further in lessons to come.

You'll also take several surveys and self-assessments throughout the course. This will help us (and you) get a sense of how you're doing.

The minimum number of postings needed to maintain a healthy online community will vary from model to model, depending on the number of participants, the number of facilitators and/or instructors, and the nature of the assignments. In the TLC, one comment per week is considered marginal, while two to three are expected. Of course, posting more frequently is certainly welcome.

In addition, there should be evidence in the postings that participants are reading one another's comments — that is, the participants should make references to each other's points of view. In INTEC, this value is reflected in the following rubric:

POINT VALUE	CHARACTERIZATION OF THE RESPONSE
0	No response.
1/2	Single entry; no interaction with other participants' postings is evident
1	The response builds on the ideas of another one or two participants and digs deeper into assignment questions or issues.
2	The response integrates multiple views and shows value as a seed for reflection by including other participants' views

Participants may, of course, respond more than the required number of times. The grading, however, is weighted toward contributions that build deeper reflection.

Using such a rubric, students are challenged to post in a way that encourages them to build upon each other's comments. The result is higher-quality dialogue, because participants value contributions — especially those that integrate the comments of others — as part of their grade.

The Online Community Meets Its Members' Needs, and Participants Express Honest Opinions

In a healthy online learning community, there is intellectual trust among participants and the facilitator. Evidence of this trust shows up in participants' apparent willingness to take intellectual risks, and to make corrections where needed so that no one is misinformed.

The participant in the example below obviously feels comfortable enough with the facilitator to express her honest opinions about several aspects of the course:

> **Re: Work and Stuff**
> **Comment to: Are the TLC Workload**
> **and Schedule Reasonable?**
>
> Hi [Moderator]! At first I thought that the work was going to be overwhelming, but that was mostly because the program felt very awkward to me. Now that I know my way around more, the expectations feel very manageable, although I still find Lotus Notes to be rather cumbersome to use (slow and not very efficient). I also think that the course *feels* better now that it is in use rather than in theory, if you know what I mean. I also decided that I was not going to let the volume of work stress me out, because then it wouldn't be any fun. I decided to do what I could, when I could, as best as I could. In this light I'd like to say that I really appreciate the feedback I have gotten, but I feel that I could use more. I try to "check in" daily and comment wherever I can, but I never know if it's enough, or if anybody reads what I write (I only feel this way in my more vulnerable moments). I just think a little more reinforcement about quantity and quality would be appreciated. I feel better already.

To facilitate a netcourse effectively, you need to know that the online community is meeting its members' needs. For this to happen, the participants need to feel empowered to honestly give you their opinions of the course.

The facilitator in the example below encourages participants to send feedback and to ask for help if they're feeling confused.

> If at any time you start to feel lost or behind in the course, don't panic or keep silent — let us know so we can help! If we don't hear from you, we'll assume you're up to date; we won't know you're having trouble.

This facilitator stresses that open and clear communication is at the heart of the netcourse community. She uses this introductory document to encourage participants to feel comfortable asking questions and sharing their thoughts with the entire community. She tries to put participants at ease about any insecurities they may have regarding posting in this new community, and she also tries to address "shy" members immediately.

The TLC "Student Guidelines" document (below) outlines the course's flexibility and responsiveness to participants' feedback and needs:

> One of the most important aspects of a netcourse is good communication. This is needed for us to be good instructors and for you to learn as much as possible.

> Please feel free to ask any of us questions about the VHS, LearningSpace, or specific assignments. At first, you'll be using email. Then, in Week 2, you'll enter questions within the course.

> Don't be shy about asking what may seem to be a really stupid question. We also want to hear questions about things already covered, that you just didn't get the first time, or maybe forgot the answer to. Others will likely have the same questions and be grateful you brought them up.

> Please let us know if we need to make adjustments to our communication styles. Are we going too fast? Too slow? Are we being too techie?

This is a biggie: This TLC course isn't set in stone. We want to know which formats and layouts work, what styles you prefer, and what things just don't work for you. (Extra points go to those who find typos or misinformation!) Keep us continually posted on what you're thinking and how's it going for you.

For trust to grow, participants in a healthy community feel heard and acknowledged. Even heated discussions may occur without "flaming" — the Internet's version of personal attacks — if participants are respectfully challenged on their ideas, not their personalities.

Participant-to-Participant Collaboration and Teaching Are Evident, and Spontaneous Moderating Occurs among the Participants

In any moderated online setting, it's likely that you, the facilitator, will be posting questions to the group. However, in addition to such typical exchanges, you'll find in both the TLC and INTEC that plenty of questions are initiated by the participants themselves, and that those questions are directed not only at the facilitators but also at their coparticipants. The questions can be technical, navigational, content focused, or even personal in nature.

Additionally, you'll often see words of encouragement and acknowledgment posted by the participants. This spontaneous "moderating" by the participants is another sign that a healthy online community is developing.

Spontaneous facilitation will emerge if the participants feel they're part of a supportive community that is engaging in a learning process together. The participants (including you and any other facilitators) should feel they're all striving toward a common goal rather than competing against each other. You can foster this type of collaborative environment by stressing joint inquiry into all aspects of the course, and by creating small "support groups" or teams around long-term assignments. How? Well, some courseware allows you to actually create private team discussions. Or, without going that far, you could put people together (e.g., "Marsha, Harry, and Gene, you three be sure to read each other's outlines and offer each other feedback"). You'll achieve your goals as facilitator and truly become a "Guide on the Side" by helping participants actively respond to each other with questions, ideas, and advice.

There are a variety of approaches you can use to foster wider, collegial exchanges among the participants. You could, for instance, build co-moderating tasks into your assignments. Or, you could have the participants take turns facilitating in a series of meetings.

You could also build various approaches into the course design to ensure that acknowledgment and feedback come from multiple sources (i.e., the participants' peers, not just you and the other facilitators). Here are a few specific ideas, from the TLC and INTEC, for doing just that:

Multiple "expert" facilitators. It may be useful to have more than one facilitator in an online community. That way, participants receive encouragement from multiple sources, and the burden of responding to the many posts doesn't fall on one person.

The TLC has one main facilitator and one secondary facilitator, as well as several faculty members who act as facilitators around their particular areas of expertise. For example, one facilitator focuses on technical issues, another on content issues, another on administrative issues, and so on. This setup allows the main facilitator to share his or her duties, and it lets each participant get feedback from the most knowledgeable source(s).

The INTEC design includes "Field Experts," who join the primary facilitators when participants try a new tool (e.g., software or a math manipulative) in their classrooms. These additional moderators bring expertise to the dialogue. They are experienced teachers who have already used the same new tool with their own students in the classroom.

Building in technical expertise or a mentor for your group to query and challenge can greatly enhance collaboration among the participants by drawing out commentary that they might not otherwise explore.

Buddy groups with mentors. In the TLC, small "buddy groups" of two or three participants and one TLC graduate (acting as a mentor/facilitator) are established midway through the course, just as the students start designing their own netcourses. The main TLC facilitator still acknowledges all work, but in addition each participant has one or two peers and one mentor committed to giving him or her feedback and support.

These smaller, focused groups are particularly conducive to student-shared facilitation and student-initiated dialogue. They provide a comfortable space in which students can practice peer review, ask questions of each other, and start work-related discussions.

And, of course, this format also allows TLC graduates to serve as mentors for a later course.

Small, student-facilitated discussion groups. If you can't bring in lots of experienced mentors or co-facilitators for your netcourse, another possibility is to group the participants into smaller numbers and assign student facilitators from within each group. The moderating duty can rotate so that all of the students have at least one opportunity to facilitate.

The best group size in this situation, as it turns out, is somewhat larger than the face-to-face ideal of three or four. Even eight works well. In the TLC, we ask students to read about moderating and fostering participation before we assign them to lead their team discussions (which they do for a week at a time). The discussion topics are always structured around an assigned lesson. (For example, "Standards for Netcourses" is a student-led discussion in the TLC.) But it's up to the students to think about how to develop an in-depth dialogue, and to try out different techniques for encouraging participation among their peers.

The first TLC had over thirty teachers (and an additional twenty site coordinators) participating at once. As the community grew, and as the assignments and the use of new technology became more intense, the number of postings quickly escalated to an overwhelming quantity. Participants could barely keep up with reading the discussion posts, never mind posting their own additional responses. It became clear that we needed to divide the community into smaller, more manageable clusters of participants.

So we split the TLC into three groups of ten participants, with each group having a faculty facilitator. The groups were focused around the main goal of the TLC: Each participant's development of a high school netcourse. Participants within each group were expected to post their course outlines and plans and to give feedback on the outlines of the other members in their group. Participants were free to look at the other groups' postings, but they weren't required to.

In the end, this structure freed up participants. The results: Increased back-and-forth dialogue between the peers, and more collaboration in their netcourse designs. Additionally, the participants in each small group grew closer and established a tight support structure for themselves.

Hybrid model. The INTEC project has experimented with combining the online course with local face-to-face meetings. Districts or schools that joined INTEC were asked to show that they were already part of a school- or district-wide effort to embrace inquiry in their mathematics and science curricula. The impact of this approach: Teachers must work offline with their colleagues on the materials presented in the course.

Instructors and students alike have found this model to be a powerful one. Members of each face-to-face local group take turns leading the meetings, further sharing the role of facilitating but doing so in more familiar (face-to-face) territory.

Social collaboration. How can one tell that an online community such as the TLC has really become an active collaboration? By looking at, in our case, the "Water Cooler" discussion area.

We established the Water Cooler specifically as a place where participants can get to know each other, share personal stories, and just plain have fun. However, there is also a great deal of spontaneous sharing, helping, and learning that occurs among participants within this space. Because they feel they're part of an exciting and supportive team of joint learners, participants use the Water Cooler space to start collaborating and offering advice to each other outside of their assigned lessons.

Once, as part of an assignment that asks TLC participants to start playing with graphics and attachments, a group spontaneously assembled, within the Water Cooler space, a graphical representation of a teacher's lounge. One person contributed a picture of donuts, another a picture of a coffeepot, and still another a picture of a soda machine. During this lengthy discussion thread, the participants played, experimented, and shared their knowledge to help each other master what, for many, were such novel technical skills as opening, attaching, viewing, and saving graphical files over the Web. The participants who had figured out how to attach and view graphics talked the others through the process. And they did it in a way that was fun and brought the participants closer together as a community — they did it in a metaphorical "teacher's lounge!" The comforting, welcoming image of the teacher's lounge allowed the participants to feel they were in a familiar, common space where they could talk, share, and get to know each other.

This example of participant-to-participant teaching stemmed from the simple creation of a Water Cooler discussion area. The participants themselves initiated the teacher's lounge discussion thread after one of the facilitators posed a simple challenge asking if anyone knew how to open an attachment.

How can you encourage this level of enthusiastic, participant-to-participant teaching in your netcourses? By acknowledging and giving a "good job" or a "thanks" to a student who helps another student. If one participant is well versed in an area that others are struggling with, and if you encourage that participant as he or she shares knowledge, then all of the participants will become more comfortable taking on the facilitator's role at times. So instead of answering all questions right away, readdress some of them to the group as a sort of challenge, to see if the community can arrive at a conclusion together — with the more knowledgeable members leading the way.

The following is an example of peer teaching and learning in the TLC. Each participant had posted a draft outline for the high school netcourse he or she was developing. After the outlines were posted, students were given a structured assignment: Each participant had to read and respond to three of his or her peers' outlines, giving constructive feedback and advice. The three comments below were written by students for a fellow classmate, in response to his outline:

Comment 1

Hi,

This is such an important course. We tend to take water for granted, especially in the area where I live. We have a rich aquifer, and few people question if there will be a time when we don't have safe drinking water. I'd like to believe that people from other areas, like our SW, have a more enlightened view. It sounds like you have planned lots of great activities along with writing and reading assignments. Have you considered trying to incorporate "The Cadillac Desert"? I can't remember the author's name at the moment, but I recall that this is a book that led to a six-week PBS series. It was really interesting, but I'm not sure if it would fit your course and I don't know how you would get it to your students.

Another idea is to include indicator species that help us determine the pollution level of freshwater systems.

I may have to borrow some of your ideas for my Field Biology class. We'll be studying water this spring.

[Coparticipant]

Comment 2

Hi,

This looks good. I think that most of us don't realize the importance of water in our daily life. On PBS this morning I heard a statement ... "Land won't be the problem in the production of food for the future, but water will." That's interesting to think about. I would like to get some input from you as I develop the segment of my course that looks at water resources.

Thanks,

[Coparticipant]

Comment 3

I was attracted by the course title: "Water and the World." The welcome part of the course outline is the most interesting, as water supply is an issue that is of much concern to my country, Singapore. We have a small water catchment area and have to buy water from our neighbors. There are many interesting activities in this course that I believe many of my students would love to participate in: Writing, experimenting, analysis, comparing, surveying, investigating, etc.

Some questions:

In Week 5, students are asked to write a report on purification. Does that mean there is only one method, chemical purification? Are there alternatives? (See Week 11.)

In Weeks 8 and 13, will there be reading articles in the Media Center on coliform bacteria, chlorine, hardness?

[Coparticipant]

Reasonable Venting about Technology, Content, and Even the Facilitator, Is Acceptable and Evident

Venting will be most productive to the community if the "ventor" feels his or her frustrations have been heard and acknowledged by you and the other participants, and that the venting may bring some change.

As facilitator, you should respond to any post in which the participant is frustrated. And be sure to have patience with participants who vent a lot!

The following exchange shows that reasonable venting is preferable to silent nonparticipation. Of course, you may have to establish some limits if the venting takes on an inappropriate tone or is harassing in any way:

Participant:

Can someone help me get a grip on this annotation thing? I don't have any clue as to what I'm doing or where I'm supposed to start, and I think that annotation is going to be a big part of my course so that I can comment on specific pieces of literature ... HELP!

The participant here is obviously frustrated with one of the assignments.

Facilitator:

Hi,

I applaud you for stepping out and asking questions! But why are you asking about annotations when I see an annotation for you already in Week 2?

In any event, here is more info for the Week 2, Lesson 8 assignment. You should go to the Media Center. When you first open the TLC, you should have seen four pictures representing different databases (Schedule, Profiles, CourseRoom, MediaCenter.) Click on ...[long technical explanation follows] ... Hope this helps!

The facilitator's positive response makes it clear that all questions and problems are welcomed, and that the instructors would rather hear about any and all problems than have participants stay quiet when they're confused.

Participant:

Hi,

Thanks so much for the help. I commented before I really got down into the meat of the Media Center assignment. I really was frustrated and needed to vent ... I have done three weeks of TLC in 1 1/2 weeks because my hard drive went in for an upgrade and a memory boost just about the time this course started ... I got to the annotations about midnight and I got confused ... When I got back to the lesson the next day, it was as clear as crystal what I was supposed to do ... Again, thanks for the shoulder to cry on.

The participant acknowledges that she was frustrated and was "venting," but the support she received obviously meant a great deal to her. Now she's ready to move on.

If you don't encourage this type of exchange, participants may become paralyzed with frustration and quietly fade away until someone notices their absence.

Participants Show Concern and Support for the Community

Setting a tone of concern and support for members of the virtual community nurtures the feeling of safety we discussed earlier. This tone setting can take on several forms.

Given the text-based format of the community gathering space, what the text looks like can become part of the message. The following is a typical example, from the first TLC. An instructor had submitted a post titled **"I WANT SOME TLC."** The title of his message was in bold face. (In the medium of LearningSpace, you can easily present bold, italic, and even font changes.) He was seeking feedback from participants on whether or not they were feeling overwhelmed. Here's what he asked the participants to do:

> Go to the "Water Cooler" under my new topic, **"I WANT SOME TLC,"** and tell us how much time you're spending on this per week and whether it's too much. I WANT TO SEE 30 RESPONSES IN THERE!

The conversation that ensued was not at all what the instructor had intended, though everyone learned a great deal as a result. One participant responded quickly:

FROM: [Participant]

RE: Stop Yelling at Me

[Facilitator],

I just started feeling major pangs of regret for not spending nearly enough time in the TLC. I guess that's why I'm only a site coordinator.

Frankly, I need, like, a gazillion hours to look at all the stuff that I have neglected. And I plan to do just that this weekend!

[Participant]

This participant had obviously interpreted the moderator's enthusiastic use of bold and capitalized letters as him "yelling" at her — an interpretation the moderator did not at all intend.

The participant interpreted the phrase in bold face — **"I WANT SOME TLC "** — as a demand by the course instructor, not as a social comment inviting participants to air any problems or gripes they might have. The "I" in "I WANT" was intended, in one sense, not in reference to the moderator but to the TLC participant and his or her voicing needs for support. The ambiguity of "TLC" as standing for either "Teacher Learning Conference" or "Tender Loving Care," though creative and potentially inviting, also likely caused confusion.

Intonation and gesture in a face-to-face meeting would easily have carried this ambiguous meaning. Not so in the online environment, as this leader discovered. Perhaps the results would have been different if he'd phrased his post something like this:

> "We're all putting in a lot of time, perhaps too much. We all could use some TLC (Tender Loving Care) in our TLC (Teacher Learning Conference) ;-). Can folks go to the Water Cooler and look at the thread I put up, *I WANT SOME TLC,* meaning Tender Loving Care, and put up suggestions on how we can help? By the way, the CAPS are for emphasis, not yelling."

The use of capital letters in the original post, intended both to emphasize and honor the needs of the participants, was instead interpreted as yelling. The guilt evoked by the moderator's entry also invited a common complaint (e.g., "I need, like, a gazillion hours ... "). Processing ideas always takes more time than one originally plans. Evoking an unintended effect of generating more guilt rather than easing the burden of feeling overworked demanded further time and effort on the part of this facilitator in both private emails and the public forum. In a face-to-face dialogue, you can rapidly clear up such misunderstandings. But online, misunderstandings take considerably longer to fix, and they consume inordinate amounts of precious resources — including time, energy, and goodwill.

You must always pay careful attention to potential misreadings of social communications, and be prepared for the possibility that participants will be confused by your assignments or directives. An important caveat to remember is that the effective tone of a post is not what you *intend* it to be, but what a participant *perceives* upon reading it. Something you intend as helpful or cheery can easily be misinterpreted, in the text format, as scolding, directive, or even sarcastic:

FROM: [Moderator]

RE: Not Yelling, Just Helping

... Did that really feel like yelling?

Sorry ... It was meant to be empathetic, sensitive, and caring.

The facilitator responded publicly, attempting to clear up problems and redirect the interactions by apologizing and changing the message subject. The facilitator also sent the participant a private email.

FROM: [Another Participant]

RE: Capital Letters = Yelling in Netspeak

Hard to modulate the voice, isn't it, when you only have a choice of upper and lower case. I'm looking forward to the day when we can use fonts in email: Lucinda Handwriting or Future Script for soft politeness, and IMPACT for firmness. San Francisco for teasing and joking. Juniper for swearing. Courier for droning.

[Another Participant]

Another participant, more experienced in net communications, joins the conversation and tries to clarify. The participant cites the limitations of text-based interactions, then makes possible, though impractical, suggestions that reinforce the care everyone must take to communicate their true intentions.

The dialogue in this netcourse eventually got back on track, but only after some precious resources had been used ineffectively.

Special threads in both the social and academic areas of a netcourse can contain FAQs (Frequently Asked Questions) about common issues relating to *emoticons* (keyboard symbols used to express a participant's emotions) and *'netiquette* (Internet etiquette). Other FAQ threads can address process issues — such as expectations for responses, or the appropriate use of personal and staff resources — and help participants make the transition from what is commonly *social* dialogue in early assignments to *active engagement* with ideas and collaborative learning.

There will always be some newcomers to netcourses. FAQ threads crafted to suit particular course or group needs can serve an important function. Time devoted to explaining basic 'netiquette, net civility, and more general issues of process or expectations is time well spent.

Below is a sample FAQ document in the 'netiquette thread. It isn't too preachy, and it keeps the subject positive and fun with the inclusion of the emoticon examples:

RE: Keep Your Voice Down — Using CAPS to Emphasize

USING ALL CAPITAL LETTERS is the equivalent of yelling. Ouch!

Instead, use asterisks — for example, *definitely* — around text you want to emphasize.

Avoid sarcasm and subtleties.

Hearing spoken words and seeing people's faces and bodies while they talk versus only reading dialogue on your computer screen can convey substantially different impressions. It's very easy to sound insensitive and to hurt someone's feelings or have them miss the point. It's good to express your opinions in discussions, but don't make disagreements personal.

Make communications with the others friendly and positive.

Remember that things you type are recorded and saved.

Emoticons, or "smileys," are helpful. These little fellas are more than just cutesy; they're actually quite effective in supplying primitive "facial expressions" to supplement your words. Tilt your head to the left to "read" each facial expression below:

:-)	basic smile
:^)	basic smile, version 2
:-P	tongue out
:-(	frown
8-)	looking out at you from your monitor
=)	glazed-over (from typing? learning?)
;-)	wink
:-D	big smile
:-o	oh, no!
:-z	oh dear!

Sharing Documents Online

Another issue that can impact a participant's perception of the tone or friendliness of the discussion can be termed *software version civility*. If your discussion space permits sharing attachments, version incompatibility will surely arise at some point. Unless you've planned for it well in advance as part of your course design, it's unlikely that all of your participants will be working with the same version of a word processor or another application. You can alleviate a great deal of alienation and frustration by having a FAQ document that explicitly deals with saving in a commonly readable format like .txt (text-only) or .rtf (rich-text format), or agreeing to "save as" in an earlier version of an application that all participants can read.

Another part of software version civility involves paying attention to different compression algorithms (i.e., Zip, BinHex) for compressed files, or to different image formats (e.g., .pic, .jpg, .gif). A technical FAQ should alert new users to the potential problems and encourage them to use compression tools or image converters that everyone can decode, so that everybody feels they're "in the loop."

A Caring Community

Mutual support and civility — in terms of both netiquette in general and versions of software specifically — must be proactively structured and managed in a course space. Otherwise you'll consume valuable energy that would be better directed toward online dialogue as community members bring all kinds of agendas to their new virtual colleagues.

Support and concern is critical for fostering a sense of safety among your participants. But there must also be limits ensuring the general health and productivity of the group. In the following discussion, for example, participants and one of the facilitators posted messages of concern and support in response to a peer who was behind on his assignment due to a personal conflict at home. Clearly, an intimate and supportive community can be built online among people who have never met each other face to face. Note especially how the facilitator's post (the last one) offers support but also gently guides the discussion back to topic at hand:

Other Than That, How Was the Play, Mrs. Lincoln?

I was just congratulating myself on how easily it had gone — everything in my outline had slipped easily into the Notes format, with no technical glitches! Of course, everything looked very sparse — usually nothing but titles, where whole days of work should be, but at least the technology was under control. So I was just about to post this comment, a week ago today, when my principal called and told me I was needed in the office of our Middle School.

I went over there, and that principal told me that my son had been expelled from school, and that because of what he had done, state law required that he could not be readmitted for one year! At that moment, my wife was on a plane, headed for Las Vegas to do her duty as president of the Washington State Science Teachers Association at the National Science Teachers Convention, so it was all up to me.

Needless to say, TLC went on the back burner for a while. It had sort of a happy ending, though. I (reluctantly) put on my lawyer hat again, and found out that the law had been misinterpreted, and that my son's actions, even if as represented, did not require expulsion — in fact, expulsion was not even possible if any other solutions were possible. This, plus his prior discipline record (only one out-of-class referral in three years), made it possible to get him back into school with only five days out. I even got it settled before my wife called from Las Vegas, to tell me what a terrible place it was!

So now I'm back at work on TLC, trying to add some meat into my course schedule, my wife is back home from Vegas, my son is eager to get back to school tomorrow, and we are doing a lot of family-hug-each-other stuff at home. And I'm starting to recover from the terrible cold I got in the middle of it all.

Yikes and Double Yikes
Comment to: Other Than That, How Was the Play, Mrs. Lincoln?

Hang in there ... I think that parenting is **the most difficult thing anyone can do**, even without the roadblocks, detours, etc. I think it is particularly hard when the parents are in education ... Ignorance is sometimes bliss. Remember ... you are not alone.

Yow! (and Other Things to Say When the Law Bludgeons Kids)
Comment to: Other Than That, How Was the Play, Mrs. Lincoln

[Participant]: Man, your last ten days put a lot of little glitches on this end into perspective. Glad things worked out in the end.

[Facilitator]

A Wonderful, Terrible Tale
Comment to: Other Than That, How Was the Play, Mrs. Lincoln?

Oh, you poor fella, what an ordeal you've been through.

I'm so pleased to hear that you took control of the situation, guided it to a solution that worked for you, and lived to tell. This is certainly an example of good coming from a bad situation. All except the cold.

You definitely had your priorities in order. If your course documents were already taking shape, you're still in a good place. If you find you need any help, advice, or encouragement, please ask. We're right here for you.

[Facilitator]

KEEPING AN ONLINE COMMUNITY HAPPY AND HEALTHY

Sometimes, regardless of what you do as a facilitator, the discussion area is virtually void. What then?

Time for some troubleshooting. Most commonly, facilitators face either too little or too much participation. Alternatively, there may be complaints that the course depends too heavily on participants having to build the knowledge base, or that the course is too constructive and people want answers. Still another common difficulty: The group or the group leader seems either too personal or too impersonal.

Here are a few ideas for thinking about such stumbling blocks.

There's Too Little or Too Much Participation in the Course

What does it mean when, for example, a good question gets no reply? It could mean that:

- Participants have no incentive to reply. (They haven't gotten regular feedback to their past posts from the community, or they've gotten negative feedback; or, they think posting an answer isn't required, and they'd rather focus on mandatory assignments, etc.)
- Participants are overwhelmed by the amount of work they have to do or the number of posts they have to read and respond to.
- Participants are too intimidated to be the first to post their thoughts in the thread, especially if the question is a deep one or if there have been very few participant posts in the CourseRoom.

Whatever the problem, you as the facilitator must quickly identify and address it, lest you lose critical momentum. Call, write, or visit. Low participation can be a symptom of a real problem with your virtual group or class, but it can also be simple procrastination. We have found that, in a nonrequired course, the facilitator must simply develop a critical mass of participants (at least twenty-five) and compelling content in order for the course to take off. Without an outside motivator — as in the TLC, where teachers must produce a course because students are taking it in the upcoming semester — a critical mass of participants is a must.

Perhaps surprisingly, the opposite problem can be equally dubious! If each person in a group of twenty contributes one page three times a week, everyone would have to read the equivalent of *War and Peace* over the course of a semester — in addition to what they have on the assigned reading list! So be sure to encourage short, pithy, thoughtful contributions to keep everyone optimally involved in the dialogue.

Just as you might in a physical classroom, you'll likely discover that some participants write much more than others do. Interestingly, the "prolific" online participants are usually *not* the same people who might dominate a face-to-face group. An advantage of the text-based medium is that the rest of the class can read every word carefully or choose to scan when a post is unreasonably lengthy. If a participant consistently writes at length, without editing for content and clarity, an email reminder from you about the added power of succinct comments may curb the spill.

The Course Is Too Constructive

There is strong evidence to suggest that learners learn best when constructing their own knowledge. However, there is also a right time to clearly guide learners or simply give them a critical piece of information to help them move forward. In many cases there *are* right answers, and relying on participants to construct all of them wastes time. It may also prove frustrating at the least, if not futile.

As such, consider privately emailing the original poster of an incorrect statement. At the same time, accompany that email with an indirect public statement providing the correct information. You could do this in your next intervention, where you weave the facts into the rest of the posting. Or, you could simply restate the comments of participants who were correct and not repeat the misinformation.

The Course Is Too Personal or Impersonal

It's important to avoid direct criticism of anyone in the community if your goal is to maintain intellectual trust. Concentrate on the ideas.

So for instance, when participants contribute positively to the construction of content-related ideas, cite their contributions with their names, either by quoting or paraphrasing their valued contribution. When a participant's contribution is off track — either because the content is rejected or ignored or, alternatively, because it is content-*related* but incorrect or mistaken — you can point out the erroneous direction, but this time without "pointing a finger" at the contributor. You might use a quote or paraphrase. That way, your message can be framed something like this:

"Such-and-such feelings or beliefs are emerging in the group and need group attention, or must be acknowledged, and here's a potential route (redirection) that might be more productive."

However you acknowledge the erroneous or misdirected material, if you do so with respect and openness to clarification and you invite everyone to respond, then you bring the group to the table in a pragmatic way so that they can move forward in a direction that values and incorporates the contributions of all. You can often address the line between "too personal" (finger-pointing and/or unrealistic expectations of each member of the group) and "impersonal" (contributors aren't valued and feedback isn't offered) by something as simple as the wording of a comment.

A specific example of how minor shifts in wording can powerfully shift the frame of a message might be you following up with a nonparticipating student by sending him or her an inquiring email. The subject of the email might be, "Your Progress in INTEC." Or it could be, "Participating in INTEC." Which one would *you* rather open?

If anything in your message carries a blaming tone, the response will likely not be what you'd intended. If you're simply supportive and inquisitive, the results will be much more positive.

THE CONTINUING CHALLENGE OF MAINTAINING COMMUNITY HEALTH

The skills we present in Chapters 5 and 6 will help you further address the challenge of keeping your online community healthy, happy, and productive! Maintaining trust and encouraging risk taking among the participants in your netcourse or within your team's group work will make the endeavor most compelling and useful to everyone involved.

Ignoring the emotions participants express can be deadening. Acknowledging and honoring them can break open new levels of communication, to the benefit and enrichment of the entire group. Exploring them too far, on the other hand, can distract the group from its goals. The strategies that follow in Chapters 5 and 6 will be useful in helping you strike a healthy balance. Such advanced skills result in virtual communities imagined or envisioned by only a few as of yet. More people in the business of online learning believe that the route to "emotional bandwidth," or community connection beyond connectivity, will result from emulating face-to-face experiences more closely, using tools like real-time video streaming and other synchronous technologies. But participants in our work who experience the kind of skilled moderating we're about to present are usually struck by a rediscovery of the power of the written word, and by the depth of the potential for reflection in an asynchronous environment.

Skilled moderating is about serving the needs of a dialogue rather than participating appropriately in one. Those moderators who have adopted the strategies that follow have reported feeling a sense of "placelessness," meaning that, on the side, they become more like a "fifth wheel" in a functional community — being there by not being there! Given that a goal of such moderating is to encourage the group to moderate itself, the healthiest community no longer needs the moderator! Thus, the person moderating might still be serving the group in other ways (private feedback and review, for example). Once the community is skilled or mature, participants may largely take on the role of directing the dialogue themselves.

Such a conception leads us to consider how moderators get the support and feedback *they* need. This is indeed an issue that bears consideration. Teams of moderators can form cohesive communities themselves, or such supporting structures can be institutionalized by an organization engaged in supporting online learning or teamwork. The pyramid model, which we described in Chapter 3, lends itself to structuring support for facilitators who are implementing the advanced moderating strategies described in the pages that follow.

Chapter Five

■ ■ ■ ■ ■ ■ ■ ■ ■

VOICE

■■■■■■ INTRODUCTION

There are two general classes of "strategies" you must master as the facilitator of an online discussion group. The first — "Basic and General 'Netiquette" — should be familiar to you if you've taken or taught online courses before or participated in a work-related virtual collaboration.

The term *'netiquette* was coined to describe the online equivalent of politeness or civility in the day-to-day physical world. We extend the definition of general 'netiquette to include:

- Strategies and mechanisms for setting the tone in online discussions
- Elements like humor or emotions to infuse personality into discussions
- Effective transitions from social dialogue to more substantive interactions
- The use of non-text supports, such as multimedia, to build the sense of being in a physical classroom
- The collegiality needed to support and sustain pragmatic dialogue online

As we've pointed out in previous chapters, using these basic moderating strategies successfully will help you see how virtual communities can be both functional and constructive environments for learning. However, these strategies might also pose for you significant challenges related to maintaining the health and productivity of your community. That's why, as a "Guide on the Side," you must also learn more advanced dialogue strategies, so that you can have the best chance of bringing Internet teaching forward as a valuable way to support virtual learning communities.

By using these advanced tactics effectively, you'll move your community's dialogue toward set goals while avoiding interventions that keep you standing in the middle (or in the way) or being perceived as owning or directing the discourse — thus inadvertently reducing the responsibility of participants for their own learning. Accomplished discussion leaders in the physical classroom bring myriad practiced approaches to their work. Many of these approaches — particularly if they're based on visual or aural cues, the leader's personal presence, or even the leader's charisma — don't survive translation to a text-based forum. Analysis of the work of experienced online discussion moderators reveals that each moderator brings to the craft a limited set of strategies for engagement with ideas, and very few "voices" or "personas" that convey his or her comments.

This chapter and the two that follow (Chapters 6 and 7) present a schema of six *critical-thinking strategies*, along with a palette of options for *voice* and *tone* from which you, the moderator, may select to achieve specific effects for your intervention. We have derived these strategies and voices from the literature on dialogue, recent work in critical thinking, and experimentation with and observation of the work of talented moderators in both the TLC and INTEC.

The *advanced strategies for moderation,* as we label them, are analogous to the protocols for nondirective interviewing and questioning of clients used by psychologists, counselors, and social workers. These strategies may seem artificial and limiting at first glance. But experienced moderators tell us that these schema give them completely new ways to envision entering and interacting with a dialogue. Moderators who are comfortable with the voice of a *Personal Muse* or a *Mediator*, for instance, see ways to compose posts as *Reflective Guides* or as *Role Plays* so that they can highlight dialogue elements they could not previously address. Some moderators have even remarked that their own natural written voices, once so comfortable, have now become one of a palette of many different options at their disposal.

By paying attention to critical-thinking strategies, you can frame your posts as clarifying or focusing on important points, highlighting connections, or uncovering tensions. And you can thus move discussion forward so that participants have a deeper engagement with ideas.

Let us now briefly explore the palette of *voices* and *tones* — as well as the six *critical-thinking strategies* — we've been using successfully to foster online learning that is both compelling and lasting.

The Landscape of Advanced Moderating Skills

Traditional leadership roles — lecturer, workshop leader, or individual or small-group tutor — don't translate effectively to the environment of an asynchronous dialogue. These roles are simply too teacher-oriented. They also consume an inordinate amount of staff time as the leader interacts with the participants who are attempting to master material.

As the moderator of an online course or work group, while you build and maintain a sense of community and the open sharing of ideas, you also need to attend to the central goal: You must keep the intellectual content of the dialogue *moving forward*. To help you as the "Guide on the Side" in this regard, we've developed a palette of six *voices*, eight *tones*, and six *critical-thinking strategies* that permit you to author targeted interventions addressing specific issues. These tools focus and polish, or extend and deepen, the ideas that appear in your group's dialogues.

The time you give to analyzing and composing your interventions will always be a precious commodity. This set of voices, tones, and critical-thinking strategies offers limited but highly effective protocols that will contain and guide your compositions. In our experience, we've seen that most moderators, even practiced ones, approach the craft of moderating with a limited set of conceptual tools. The palette of voices and tones, coupled with the set of detailed critical-thinking strategies, offers a wider suite of options for you to help you write effective interventions. And while all of these tools may seem out of the ordinary at first, you can learn them pretty easily.

Here's a brief look at the voices, tones, and critical-thinking strategies we'll discuss in the rest of this chapter and in Chapters 6 and 7:

VOICES	TONES		CRITICAL-THINKING STRATEGIES
Generative Guide	Nurturing	Imaginative	Strategies that sharpen focus
Conceptual Facilitator	Curious	Informal	
Reflective Guide	Humorous	Neutral	Strategies that dig deeper
Personal Muse	Analytical	Whimsical	
Mediator			
Role Play			

When using these advanced strategies, you must first decide on a rationale for posting. Perhaps, for example, your group is in an introductory, social phase, or it's "wallowing in the shallows" of the content. Or maybe your group's online discussions include some posts that, collectively, contain some fine material you'd like to separate from the diffuse or chatty matrix. In these two cases, you may want to choose a particular critical-thinking strategy and combine it with a certain voice and/or tone so that you can highlight the important ideas in the discussion(s).

A particular discussion may have an extensive set of entries, yet harbor parallels, hidden assumptions or beliefs, or potential tensions that may not be evident to the participants. As the moderator, you can select one of the three critical-thinking strategies that *push dialogue deeper.* And from the palette of six voices, you can choose one voice that aligns with both the rationale of your post and the context of the dialogue.

In any process of online facilitation, all elements — voice, tone, and critical thinking strategy — are simultaneous. The medium of text, however, forces a linear exploration of the palette of voices and the critical-thinking strategy framework. So for the purposes of illustration, we begin in this chapter with an examination of the palette of voices.

A PALETTE OF VOICES

After you decide upon when and where to craft an intervention, or upon your rationale for intervening, you're ready to select an appropriate voice. The use of "voice" in the context of facilitating online goal-directed dialogue differs significantly from the "voice" of narrative or expository text or other literary forms of communication. The voice of the author in the more traditional forms is a vehicle to entertain, amuse, challenge the imagination, socialize, pass time pleasantly, or support vigorous debate or argument. For this type of author, the voice expresses his or her personal perspectives or creative visions. We can often recognize, in unattributed passages, the voices of authors like William Faulkner or Maya Angelou. The voice of a *New York Times* editorial or a philosophical essay is equally recognizable. These literary or expository voices speak to us for particular reasons.

In contrast, the voice of an online moderator who is a "Guide on the Side" serves a very specific need. The goal of the moderator's communication is not the expression of a personal or creative vision; rather, it is to clarify and extend the thinking of *other people*. To this end, the moderator selects a voice, which may or may not feel comfortable, to help the participants see their own thinking for a specific time or context in the dialogue. Thus, the voice in this context is really a tool that facilitates others' reflections and pre-presentations of their ideas, with the purpose of moving the dialogue or learning forward.

Much like a talented classroom instructor or meeting facilitator would, you, as the leader of an asynchronous text-based group, must command the use of many different voices to achieve and support effective interactions in various online discussions. Both online and off, your voice reflects a certain diagnosis of the group and what it needs next to most effectively maintain forward movement toward agreed upon goals or objectives. In a face-to-face situation, this diagnosis is more like ongoing "micro-diagnoses" as the dialogue and visual cues shift and change. ("They're getting tired or bored, time to insert a joke," or, "They're tossing the baby out with the bathwater here, time for a story," etc.) For a talented facilitator or instructor, this work is subconscious — or, as we more commonly say, it just "comes naturally."

In an asynchronous text-based environment, on the other hand, the diagnosis or voice must be more deliberate, especially at first. It is based on the accumulated "chunk," if you will, of dialogue that has been posted since your last point of intervention. You then pinpoint a ration-ale for an intervention ("What will help this group move forward?") by identifying the rich learning opportunities in the text, the evident tensions or gaps in the thinking of the group members, and unresolved key issues.

As you learn to identify patterns in text, you'll also come to see how the written word or the graphically organized page can provide alternatives to the body language, facial gestures, and voice inflections that mediate face-to-face discussions. Paralleling classroom gestures and visual and aural exchange, the voices you use as the facilitator will provide bridges between where a class or group is and where it needs to go — by both highlighting and guiding.

We've identified six voices that will support you in the role of "Guide on the Side" — one who clarifies and reveals the thoughts of the participants to themselves. This framework is not exhaustive or even unique — we put it forward as the set we've simply found to be most useful. The voices are:

- Generative Guide
- Conceptual Facilitator
- Reflective Guide
- Personal Muse
- Mediator
- Role Play

Most experienced moderators engage participants with, at most, three different voices. Moderators with training in psychology or social science, for instance, will often write with attention to personal reflection and mediation. Other moderators, with backgrounds in academics, the sciences, or management, tend to approach the task with attention to exploring concepts or focusing on conceptual tensions. As a "Guide on the Side" moderator, you must try to hold up, for examination by both individuals and the group, the individuals' own thoughts. To do so, you need this full palette of voices, so that you can represent ideas more clearly, juxtapose ideas precisely, and show how ideas can be applied more effectively. Expanding your personal palette of "tools," or voices, then, will increase your skill in serving the needs of any dialogue you facilitate.

To use this wide palette, first examine a dialogue for rich areas of exploration or further dialogue. Then look over this framework to get an idea of what voice might most effectively address the need that is evident.

Here are the six voices in detail, as well as some examples illustrating them.

Generative Guide

Professional jargon frequently honors the timeworn; the newest buzzwords can flash in and out of postings without critical examination. Dialogues can also stagnate for lack of fresh approaches to recurring issues or positions.

As the facilitator assuming the voice of a *Generative Guide*, you may wish to lay out a spectrum of current or possible positions taken to indicate avenues of questioning that have remained overlooked or unexplored. If little has been posted, this may mean simply reiterating the posting assignment, perhaps with a fresh take. If your diagnosis is that plenty has been posted but little of value has been revealed, your job then is to identify segments of a dialogue that are confined by language or by the conceptual frameworks of their contributors. You also can list current directions or contributions, and seek alternative ordering principles, extensions, or interpretations, with the goal of targeting likely conceptual blocks or assumptions. Using critical-thinking strategies that push deeper, such as *full-spectrum questioning* (which we examine in Chapter 7), you may inquire in more detail about terms and assumptions the participants have tacitly agreed upon.

Here's an example of the Generative Guide strategy:

MESSAGE SUBJECT: Inquiry: "Hands-On" or "Talk"?

It's been an active week. Some roadblocks are appearing in our journey through Indoor Air, from the Global Lab unit. It might be useful to articulate some of them and see how formidable they are, or how to plan around them.

[Participant 1] voiced concerns that "it looks like lots of talking and planning and not much actual activity. I don't know if my students, or myself, are prepared for this kind of lab. How do we keep them on target?"

[Participant 2] was "underwhelmed" on opening up the package for indoor air testing. "It had odd-looking components, and the assembly instructions were not very clear. Will kids be confused and unimpressed too?"

[Participant 3] wonders whether "supplies for the CO_2 testing are limited," and "if data will be accurate."

[Participant 4] mused on experimental design for air quality: "Can kids do this? Do air temperature, humidity, and number of people act as a catalyst and increase CO_2 content? What about open doors and air flow? Too many variables to consider!"

The Indoor Air unit of Global Lab uses a large syringe to sample a quantity of air flow over a chemical indicator. It changes color on contact with CO_2.

The experimental procedure is rather simple. Design of the experiment (where and when to take the samples) is left to students, as is interpreting the data from the samples contributed by dozens of schools.

Teachers had difficulty envisioning an experiment that must be carefully thought out beforehand as well as collaborative (as it extended beyond the classroom walls).

Odd-looking equipment, confusing directions, or unfocused design can all pose problems, but these concerns might also point to a common understanding of what an inquiry "lab" is and isn't. A common model is that the same equipment is passed out to pairs or groups and the work is done in the group. Global Lab Indoor Air puts much emphasis on planning the lab, determining factors, and sharing and interpreting results over the web. The test itself takes only a few minutes. Are these expectations too far "out of the box" for your students?

"Sick room" or "sick building" are terms easily used but undefined scientifically. Associating measurable effects with specific causes should bring some understanding — or will students see this as not worth the effort?

Which locations are tested and what the testing procedure is can be scripted. What is gained by a more open design?

The moderator's composition guides teachers to think broadly about what a "lab" is and the role of planning its implementation. The burden of crafting the experimental design and evolving a coherent method of sharing data is placed on students of Global Lab. The moderator leaves participants to explore the potential gains of such a practice.

Conceptual Facilitator

Netcourse assignments or work group tasks have specific goals to achieve. In the course of a dialogue, content elements or key concepts in activities or readings may have been omitted, misconstrued, or overemphasized. As the moderator, you can assume the voice of a *Conceptual Facilitator* to address these omissions, confusions, or imbalances.

Though superficially resembling the voice of a lecturer or tutor, a Conceptual Facilitator voice focuses specifically on elements of participants' postings, perhaps including juxtapositions from readings, and not on the delivery of content material in the intervention. Thus, as the Conceptual Facilitator, you identify conceptual areas that need attention. You then attempt to point out pieces of the conceptual landscape, so that participants can fill in or adjust any that are incomplete or don't quite make sense.

As Conceptual Facilitator, you may wish to indicate current progress in the dialogue by highlighting tensions or unbalanced expositions. You can bring forward certain ideas or probe particular entries for key concepts or connections that may be missing or perhaps weakly articulated. In the voice of a Conceptual Facilitator, you can then explore participants' responses and the wording of assignments, or examine participants' usage of key concepts, citing turning points or reinterpretations. To push the dialogue even deeper, you can use analogies to explore assumptions or help clarify thinking.

Here's an example of the Conceptual Facilitator approach:

MESSAGE SUBJECT: Whole Lotta Shakin' Going on!

Or, in [**Participant 1's**] words: "Wow! It was interesting reading today!" May I second her response? I think what made today's, and the last several days', reading so interesting is that not only are many of our algebra tools group responding to playing/working with the materials and viewing the video, but we're reflecting on the meaning of these matters for our teaching and actively engaging with each other's comments. Brava and bravo.

Emboldened by [**Participant 2's**] comments on her blind student factoring with manipulatives in what seemed novel and inventive ways, and the discussion by [**Participant 3**], [**Participant 4**], and [**Participant 5**] on "fun," I'd like to offer another alternative view on doing, playing, and learning. I work with a group of English teachers who are similarly concerned with issues of fun/entertainment and the relation of these to learning. They're experimenting with teaching Shakespeare through acting as opposed to the tried-and-true (and many say failed) method of sitting

The dialogue was progressing well, as measured by engagement and volume of response, but the focus was beginning to unravel. Part of the assignment, consideration of work vs. engagement, was overlooked. The moderator elected to intervene with a post crafted to highlight main ideas both in the assignment and in the discussion area. The moderator bolds participants' names and cites their contributions.

in one's seat, analyzing, and taking tests. "Shakespeare" and "algebra" as verbs: What an idea!

What changes in learning and experience might you see when students DO algebra? "Doing" Shakespeare is not easy by any means; neither is "doing" algebra. Is challenge motivating? Or are we mixing up engagement with amusement? These two are not exclusive, certainly. How do both contribute to learning? Or is one more supportive?

I look forward to hearing what y'all have to think on these matters.

The ideas of having fun, doing something, being challenged, and engaging or working on something were not adequately separated out. The voice of the moderator as Conceptual Facilitator, using a metaphor from another discipline, guides participants to juxtapose ideas of enjoyment and engagement and consider how each may separately contribute to learning.

Reflective Guide

The *Reflective Guide* restates or recrafts, with slightly different emphasis, the elements of a message or sequence of messages. A Reflective Guide posting carries a sense of non-directive interaction, as effected by a Rogerian counselor, though the dialogue itself is goal-directed.

As a moderator taking this approach, you use a tone and style similar to that of the participants' postings. However, you must attempt to keep it short, and to incorporate more precise language than that found in the original posting(s). Omit irrelevant comments. Your message should retain sections of direct quotes or paraphrases of specific ideas or claims, so that participants maintain a sense of personal ownership of their entries. But you need to go beyond affirming individual participants and consider as well the group members' comprehension and direction. You can, for example, indirectly suggest similarities or perhaps tensions in the meanings of various postings; again, your role is that of a counselor or a highlighter of others' ideas.

As a Reflective Guide, you may wish to refocus dialogue around certain points or issues by selectively highlighting or paraphrasing fruitful lines of discourse. In any dialogue, there are series of entries that contain buried or poorly phrased gems. As a Reflective Guide, you may enter the dialogue modeling a voice in the recesses of the mind that seeks more precise meanings for claims or insights. You may also — both on a personal and on a more general level — include or reiterate questions about the importance of a claim. Alternatively, you may simply highlight, by inclusion and paraphrasing, any comments or insights that clarify or extend key points in the discussion. If the dialogue needs deepening rather than clarifying, you can even employ a critical thinking strategy — like exploring multiple viewpoints based on participants' responses — to model deeper layers of introspection.

Let's look at an example of how you might use the Reflective Guide approach:

MESSAGE SUBJECT:
Mulling for Meaning 2

On January 31, [Participant 1] mentions that when he attempts to add depth to his curricula instead of breadth of coverage, his science curriculum supervisor considers that as another attempt to "dumb down" what is being taught. [Participant 1] seems to feel a tension, perhaps a contradiction in this situation. "Going deeper" somehow brings up the specter of making your curriculum weaker. Is this an accurate restatement? He also feels pressures from the reform movement to go deeper into ideas. Do others feel the same tensions and pressures as [Participant 1]?

[Participant 2] wishes she'd been brought up to learn to solve problems for herself. She was raised to believe that there was one correct answer and that was that. Teachers or texts supplied that answer. We're all grappling with the issue of what it means to learn via inquiry and what it means to not have the "one right answer." [Participant 2] describes some of her struggles with her own experiences and vision of what a

The posting begins with direct references to citations and dates. Both Participant 1's and Participant 2's postings were rather lengthy. Each contained some gems of insights that needed to be brought to the surface. Both entries had similar qualities of extended reflection and self-questioning. The moderator decided to juxtapose and highlight these segments of the posts. The moderator attaches no value to the citations, other than bringing them to the group's attention.

teacher is and does. What do we bring to the "professional table," metaphorically speaking? If I understand her properly, she muses about how our unconscious belief patterns affect what we are trying to do. We all have an interest in defining for ourselves what it means to learn via inquiry. [Participant 2] has opened some new ground — looking at the unseen patterns of our own making. How do you come to terms with your own set, perhaps, of contradictory beliefs?

Hmmmm.

The Reflective Guide in this example uses paraphrasing to give more weight to the reflective segments of the postings.

Personal Muse

Reflection on practice is central to online discussion. A skilled facilitator serves as a model for the kind of reflection that pragmatic dialogue seeks to cultivate.

As a *Personal Muse*, you may craft a posting that puts forth a personal internal dialogue about central issues. In other words, you hold your own beliefs up to question. You can carefully craft a Personal Muse posting to exhibit tensions or dilemmas around which your reflection revolves, with citations from participants being your starting point. You then hold up assumptions and examine possible reasons for either holding onto or discarding them.

The Personal Muse approach models, in a public forum, the kind of internal dialogue anyone might have with himself or herself when critically examining his or her beliefs. There is a fundamental commitment to pragmatic, rather than argumentative, dialogue; there is no "winner."

It's important that the questions you express in the voice of a Personal Muse be presented as parts of assignments. They are rhetorical artifacts, asked and answered for the purpose of modeling open exploration of ideas.

Particular instances that suit a Personal Muse intervention include dialogues that show evidence of slowing down or getting muddled. As Personal Muse, you can attempt to renew the discussion or redirect its energy without engaging or confronting individuals directly. You could, for instance, muse about how to distinguish relevant from irrelevant issues by articulating crisp analogies or recounting directions taken to date.

You can also model the process of deeper reflection for dialogues that are still caught in a shallow exploration of ideas. How? By posing and responding to a sequence of directed questions. Additionally, you might attempt to capture the process of wrestling with unresolved definitions, issues, or tensions to push ideas deeper.

One of the most important functions of the Personal Muse approach is modeling the process of suspending judgment in the spirit of inquiry, and attempting to break through barriers to new ways of thinking.

Here's an example of the Personal Muse strategy in action:

MESSAGE SUBJECT: Winter Break Musings

Hi all,

First, an apology for the delay in response. We're rediscovering winter break in the Northeast, where families either traipse off to the slopes, or the beaches, or the Science Museum.

From your comments, building the air cart seems to be a rich project. [Participant 1] shares, "The first thought I had when I was finished with the aircart was, 'How can I make it go faster?'" I know my students would come upon the same thought.

[Participant 2] remarks, "Rebuilding to have the fastest cart in the class takes time, but this is a lesson that will be remembered and has several facets to help justify the class time used on the project."

[Participant 3] adds, "When I showed the almost finished cart to my Science Club — mostly fourteen-year-olds — they immediately started to suggest

The social introduction sets an informal tone. The moderator had not intervened for a while. The dialogue space seemed to have reached a plateau of new ideas.

This entry brings to the surface participants' comments about the project from Hands On Physics: Building an Air-Powered Cart. Beyond "I liked it," there was little substantive interaction. The moderator offers no praise for specific comments, but instead incorporates them into her own musings to build context for further reflection. There is a strong thread of tentativeness, even self-doubt, in the composition.

---

improvements and modifications, along the lines of the suggested extensions, which impressed me. I think they could learn a lot of science from this."

[Participant 4] comments that "a design with some 'pitfalls' is helpful, as it pushes one out of the cruising mode and into a more focused, active learning mode."

My ninth-graders, for example, are not a patient lot. I wonder about relative educational value of building vs. tuning. I suspect that it is in the tuning and refining stage where the bulk of the learning will occur.

Maine, the state I'm living in, has made a big deal about aligning practice to standards, documenting our curriculum, and linking it to the state learning results. For me, that means I'm going to formally outline my major projects, the car being one of them, and show their relevance to the state and my school board. It will be a pain, but it does force me to be concrete about my purposes. I often wonder why I choose to do the projects I do, other than that I like them. I muse, "What science and learning make this car particularly valuable? Can students discover the principles of physics like Newton's second law for themselves?"

It is exciting to see all of the ideas arising out of an assembly of cardboard, glue, and simple circuitry. Or am I dreaming? I'm still struggling to make connections explicit. (Off to do some inquiry-based skiing before the snow melts.)

Mediator

Discussion entries can occasionally polarize participants, for reasons external to the content or to the group process of the community itself. Polarized dialogue often brings with it advocacy of personal positions. Defenses spring up, and the process of open dialogue slows and is in danger of dying.

By taking the role of Mediator you may use personal communication, or insights from your own experience, to assess participants' unstated reasons for their reactions. In support of the central goal — maintaining the dialogue's direction and open spirit — you redirect discussion away from defense of hardened positions and toward goals that are central to the interests of all parties. Instead of focusing on participants' articulations of their positions, you highlight their possible reasons for holding those positions. Such a transition, from a potentially argumentative forum to a pragmatic dialogue, often signals a real breakthrough for the community of learners.

You don't want to avoid the tension of argument altogether, of course; tension is essential for compelling dialogue. You simply want to redirect the tension.

At a basic level, in acting as a Mediator you can highlight similar lines of thought as well as key points echoed in the dialogue. Your "voice" in this situation may simply seek to highlight the advocacy found in a suite of posts as a potential barrier to continued pragmatic conversation. Your "voice" can then search for ways to reopen more fruitful exploration. To encourage deeper discussion, you might show a need for participants to clarify meanings or assumptions. Alternatively, you might lay out the landscape of articulated views — including those that are polarized with tension — remind participants of the original purpose and objectives (spirit?) of the dialogue, and use such regrounding to help the group move away from polarity and onto pathways of discussion that hold greater potential for growth.

Central to your function as Mediator is modeling suspension of judgment in service of clarifying issues and goals. By making connections across different levels of interpretations, you can explore suspension of belief or disbelief as potential ways of seeing a bigger picture.

Keep in mind, though, that smaller steps are more likely to enable movement among the immobilized students at any given juncture in the dialogue. As Mediator, you may have to set short- and long-term goals for the group when planning today's and future interventions. Problems that polarize are unlikely to be "solved" with a single intervention (if at all with some issues). Instead, small steps toward forward movement can set the stage for defining more common ground eventually, via a number of interventions, over time and distance.

Here's an example of how you might use the Mediator role to address a problem in online discussions:

MESSAGE SUBJECT:
Seeing and Feeling Many Ways

Three blind men and an elephant, or, perhaps, four inquiring teachers and algebra. Wow! There are so many different takes on this assignment. That's good !!! I'm reminded of the three blind men all describing the same object. "It's a snake, a tree, a rope," they cry. Controversy is a good place to start inquiry! We don't have to come to a consensus, thank heavens. We only need understand and appreciate each other's viewpoints.

[Participant 1's] reaction was mixed: "Partly I was intrigued and partly I was insulted." She sees no "right" way to teach algebra, and she wonders both about the value of the old and adding the value of the "new."

The moderator approaches the controversy with humor. Asking for reform does presume something is to be fixed.

The Mediator voice should honor all participants' views but put them in a wider context. You must set clear goals for the Mediation effort. And you must seek understanding, not consensus.

[Participant 2] is struck by a troublesome polarity with "new" materials: "It is either what we did 'way back when' or something to do besides what they are supposed to do."

[Participant 3] comments on her concern for visual or auditory learners rather than kinesthetic. She wonders if "using manipulatives takes more time than my way of doing things."

[Participant 4] remarks that teacher attitude is important. If a teacher shows satisfaction with traditional methods only, students will pick up on that mindset and will resist "new" approaches: "If it is seen as really interesting to you, they'll generally go along."

We can also consider the tale from the elephant's point of view. She's pawed and prodded by blind inquirers (researchers/reformers), for some reason unknown to her. Testiness is a natural response. [Participant 4] notes that attitudes are important. Where have you seen the most constructive changes and insights regarding new attitudes and approaches?

Notice how the moderator has streamlined participants' quotes, and highlighted the tension between advocates of old and new.

The moderator has echoed concerns about applicability and featured teacher attitude as a bridge to students' valuing an innovation.

Finally, the moderator visits the metaphor of the elephant in a different perspective and honors participants' comments. The moderator thus tries to move to issues of effectiveness.

Role Play (Character Identification)

As facilitator, you may also wish to assume a voice appropriate to one of many roles, such as the "teacher on Monday" (flush with new ideas), the "office manager on Friday" (enthusiasm chastened, yet hopeful), a time-pressured worker, or an administrator at the limit of his or her patience. Interventions in the voice of a *Role Play* may include symbolic characters, tales, or situations gleaned from your personal experiences. By using a role play or character identification in this way, you can introduce necessary alternative perspectives into the dialogue without concern for personal ownership or direct confrontation of participants.

In your role or character identification voice, you may want to indicate, through narrative means, levels of importance of the lines of thought or concepts presented. To do so, you can highlight or introduce, through characters or tales, key points that were omitted or that need reinforcing. Using critical-thinking strategies that push dialogue deeper, you can tailor your new "role" to introduce or validate multiple perspectives on key issues. You also can integrate into the main discussion ideas that may seem irrelevant but, when observed through another perspective, indicate valid and focused lines of thought.

Here's an example of a role play a moderator designed to push discussion participants out of the "shallows." In multiple postings, the previous thread had not resolved or revealed some basic assumptions blocking the participants' progress. The Role Play voice here is that of a standup comic; its tone is obviously humorous. The critical thinking strategy involves making connections:

MESSAGE SUBJECT:
Sherlock and Assumptions

A whole string of postings addresses problems relating to new ways of teaching. Some wrote a lot about block schedules, others about new pressures of testing. Still others were reviewing the time vs. coverage issue. Schedules, testing, coverage, and time will always be with us. Aren't there some new ways of looking at these old chestnuts? Are there some assumptions about importance to the process of teaching truly held in these terms that we should be examining?

The standup comic in me wants to tell an illustrative tale.

Sherlock Holmes and Watson went camping. They decided to settle down on a hilltop. Holmes asked Watson, as both reclined for the night, "Watson, what do you see?"

After a quick mention of the main ideas that seem to be recycling in the dialogue, the moderator poses a challenge to push to a deeper level of interaction and examination of assumptions.

The tale about Holmes and Watson puts in a sharp light the problem of how knowledge, training, and interpretation can obscure observation and important integration of facts.

Exercising his best deductive powers, Watson responded, "My astronomy training tells me, by the position of the stars, that it is summer and we're in the Northern Hemisphere. My knowledge of meteorology tells me it is a clear night tonight, with the potential of rain from clouds in the East. My geology training informs me that we're on a mountain that is not a volcano. The rocks seem layered and the soil is sandy. Holmes, what does your knowledge tell us about our condition?"

"Someone has stolen our tent," he responded quickly.

So where is your tent?

The tale leaves it open for participants to acknowledge the "Watson" in their own assessments to date. The missing tent metaphor can be referenced on other occasions as well.

THE POTENTIAL FOR USING VOICES

The palette of six voices presented here is not an exhaustive taxonomy of the voices or personas that are available or even advisable for you to use as a moderator. It is simply, we have found, sufficient to describe a range of approaches suitable for a very wide number of issues and problems that you'll commonly find in online discourse. The utility of the palette of voices depends greatly upon the inventiveness and skill of you, the moderator.

The parallel, mentioned previously, between schools of professional counseling and the palette of voices suggests that, rather than distancing you from your creative and constructive efforts, deliberately assuming a voice scaffolds you and supports your potential for developing a rich variety of interactions among your participants. You may doubt the value of voices like the Personal Muse, or the Reflective Guide, or, perhaps, other voices in the palette. Responses, you and other potential skeptics might say, should be crafted individually. But using the palette can actually help you do this. The palette makes you, as a message author, aware of patterns of response in your writing.

Authoring is a personal action; there's a strong tendency to use your own experiences and opinions as guides or indicators in an attempt to bring clarity to others. By consciously using *different* voices, you'll be reminded that the purpose of any composition as an online facilitator is to illuminate the thoughts of others, not to cleverly or entertainingly craft a position that puts you center stage. Using just *one* of the voices in any intervention narrows the content focus and places considerable demands for precision on the intent of the communication. Both constraints, we believe, are healthy for any moderated dialogue — especially since a recipient's time and attention span are limited.

Here are some avenues for checking your success at employing a "voice" in a particular intervention. To help you stay "out of the middle" at all costs, you might ask, for example:

> Did I become too didactic in this intervention? With whatever voice I selected, did the professor or unit director in my psyche intrude on the interaction and push participants with my personal take, rather than material they brought to the conversation? Or were the citations from entrants carefully chosen, clearly framed and juxtaposed to reveal tensions and avenues for more public investigation?

Often there are some gems of ideas in participants' messages, but they're well hidden and, even more commonly, undeveloped. Real insights are often buried and revealed only with hindsight. So another personal assessment you might apply to your crafting might look like this:

> Did my efforts as a moderator facilitating reflection bring the "gems" to the surface? Or did I focus too much on the grand sweep and flow of the dialogue, thus overlooking the valuable discoveries of others — from which all could have benefited?

Amidst all these voices, you're not personally "voiceless." Staying on the side does *not* mean avoiding or missing the important role of guiding the group in the direction of agreed upon goals or objectives. To this end, you might review, asking:

> In my entries, am I really modeling the kind of reflection and probing of assumptions (my own included) that this group needs to engage in? Or am I applying strategies in a formulaic way?

If the dialogue seems to you to go in circles, you want to be sure you've shown the way beyond points made and agreed upon:

> Did my attempted intervention help break patterns, or was it too forward or poorly timed? Even worse, could my entry have been perceived as supporting the same patterns that are preventing the group from thinking in new directions?

Tensions, particularly creative tensions, are essential to supporting ongoing dialogue. Have you taken full advantage of them? Ask yourself:

> Am I taking advantage of the legacy of insights and good questions from previous weeks to facilitate both individuals and the group as they explore deeper aspects of their own thinking? Or am I taking a linear approach and working with current surface details instead of being sufficiently imaginative by employing a wider conceptual pallet?

Lastly, consider your comfort level with each of the voices and the effect that might have on your group. A few of the voices described here may seem close to a "personal" writing stance or persona you use naturally. Others may seem a stretch or downright unnatural. In taking a broader view of your interventions, are there one or two voices that inform your comments? Is your personal level of comfort in stretching yourself (or not!) potentially limiting the effect your interventions might have in helping individuals and the group to see their own ideas more clearly and more deeply? Or are you able to be inventive and bold enough to go beyond your seemingly natural boundaries and write for effect to support participants' reflecting in new ways?

The palette of voices invites you to be flexible, to think beyond your own previous patterns, and to challenge your level of comfort with your writing style so that you can grow as a facilitator of the thoughts of others.

Chapter Six

■ ■ ■ ■ ■ ■ ■ ■ ■

TONE

■ WHAT DOES TONE HAVE TO DO WITH IT?

Tone is part of the triad of advanced moderating strategies largely because you're using a text-based medium where tone must be more consciously or deliberately built into one's writing. While there is certainly a "tone" to whatever someone might deliver face to face, it's an uncommon focus in "training the trainers" workshops. But it's a critical aspect of moderating as a literary genre. While the *voice* (see Chapter 5) is about "diagnosis" (i.e., "What is needed here? How do I best service this dialogue to focus and/or deepen?") and the *critical thinking strategy* (see Chapter 7) is about how to proceed (i.e., "So how do I best meet the identified need? How do I best focus and/or deepen?"), tone is a literary layer that adds dimensionality to your rationale.

As the facilitator of online dialogue, you must craft communications that are friendly, open, inviting, and polite. In terms of the usage in this book, these qualities are more accurately described as *tones*. Perhaps you recall learning the hard way at some point that it's better to maintain a positive tone in email, even when it doesn't reflect your feelings at the moment. Can you think of an example? Anger and frustration can be momentary, you might have discovered, when an email you've written with such a tone is opened by the recipient the next morning, once emotions have shifted. Problem is, now you have to calm the recipient down too — you've made things worse with your tone.

Another common occurrence: Text communication can be easier to misunderstand because the author isn't augmenting words with facial expressions. When a person makes a joke face to face, visual cues are part of the communication. Conversely, while you might be smiling as you're writing an email, the stripped-down words of your text-based communication — which seem humorous enough as you write — may not be received with the same tone, unless you add an emoticon or some extra wording that compensates for the lack of visuals at delivery.

Another common aspect of the current email culture emerges when there has been a surprising turn of events according to an email. The recipient is better off responding with a "perhaps I've missed your meaning" type of reply, to query the author instead of accusing him or her of forgetting the last mutual agreement.

What *does* work in email will work for you as a moderator as well. Positive tones disarm; they embrace and respect the thinking of all participants and foster a culture of safety for risk taking. They enhance the potential for deepened pragmatic dialogue. They keep misunderstandings to a minimum. And they can even add to the pleasure participants experience in reading your posts!

SELECTING THE TONE

As is the case in literary work or other forms of communication, the *tone* of an entry in a facilitated online discussion combines with other elements, such as voice and critical thinking strategy, to achieve an intended effect. As moderator, you select a *voice* to bring to the surface others' ideas, not as a vehicle for your own personal expression. Thus, the *tone* you select for your message must also support this end — that is, reflection.

Clearly your compositions should invite participation. Adjectives like "receptive," "thoughtful," "attractive," "comfortable," "reflective," "respectful," and "engaging" should describe all of your interventions. Going beyond your invitational role, however, you must also employ a tone that is fundamentally empathetic. Specifically, that might mean your tone could be nurturing, curious, humorous, analytical, imaginative, informal, neutral, or even whimsical. Though it's generally a good idea to assume only one voice, or to use only one critical-thinking strategy to guide a particular composition, you may use one or more tones in your postings to engage participants' interests and appeal to their imaginations.

Here's a list of specific tones we've found useful in our and others' moderating efforts. (Note: This list certainly isn't exhaustive!)

Tones

- Nurturing
- Humorous
- Imaginative
- Neutral
- Curious
- Analytical
- Informal
- Whimsical

A "neutral" tone is a baseline, and you could deliver just about any intervention that way (though such consistency gets boring after a while). In face-to-face meetings, we often turn to humor to add interest to a presentation. Since online moderating is a more literary endeavor, it seems we can even more purposefully weave humor or another tone into the mix, thus adding to both readability and to the effectiveness of the intervention — and inviting participants into further dialogue.

Above the baseline tone of neutral, analytical is a specific form of neutral that we've come to recognize. (It occurs when, quite simply, you the moderator offer an analysis with a neutral tone.)

Curious is the tone that avoids "grilling" the reader(s) with your probing question(s). You can use an informal tone in a similar way. If you sense, for example, that you're about to ask a "touchy" or pointed question, you can use an informal tone to lighten the delivery, thus making it more likely that your participants will "hear" your query.

A nurturing tone can be effective when the dialogue represents lots of hard work without too much progress (or simply lots of hard work with lots more to go). Your intent here might be to inspire a return to the difficult ground.

Whimsical, humorous, and imaginative represent the most "inspired" tones we've seen our moderators use.

Some tones may fit particularly well with certain voices or critical thinking strategies. For example, a Conceptual Facilitator might do well to be nurturing, and a Personal Muse might take a curious tone to avoid being overbearing. Note, though, that some combinations are ill-advised or strained. Trying to be a whimsical Mediator, for instance, may seem like an imaginative thing to do. But that particular tone-voice combination could instead offend either or both parties of a dispute. The parties being mediated may think you're not taking their positions seriously. Certainly these combination "rules" aren't hard and fast. Effective use of tone has much to do with the content of your message and how you use a specific tonal filter. We've seen successful Mediators build in a humorous or imaginative framework that effectively breaks down barriers.

Absent from the list are tones like "sarcastic," "threatening," and "saccharine," as it is unlikely these tones will invite further dialogue of the type you seek. Another common voice, or persona, that you may have noted as missing from our list in Chapter 5 is that of the *devil's advocate*. This form is based in argumentative dialogue; it sets up an adversarial stance that, even when well articulated, can move an active dialogue away from inquiry and toward the defense of positions. Any point you might make as a devil's advocate you could make similarly as, for example, a Personal Muse with a curious tone. Essentially all you've removed from your posting is the "edge," which would likely be experienced by readers as closed or threatening anyway.

On rare occasions, we've seen moderators effectively employ anger to stimulate dialogue. However, the moderator's anger hasn't been directed toward the participants themselves, but rather at ideas or positions in readings. The voice of a Personal Muse — modeling the possible internal dialogues of the participants — pondered the reasons behind the strong reaction described.

You may want to explore this list of tones and their fit with moderator voices by attempting to match each of the tones with a best or most comfortable fit with a voice(s). It's important to note that these tones, much like the voices described earlier, are best selected for specific times and contexts. Don't limit yourself to two or three tones, either for consistency or because they seem the most comfortable to you. Variety will add appeal for your readers, and thus make you a more effective moderator.

Chapter Seven

CRITICAL-THINKING STRATEGIES

Active engagement in critical thinking is at the core of any learning community, online or offline. While the voice and tone of your entry as moderator can provide an appealing, elegant, or illustrative surrounding for your communication, the *critical-thinking strategy* you select to frame your entry impacts the dialogue most directly.

All moderators contend with two recurring issues: Dialogues that lose focus or are conceptually murky; and dialogues that "wallow in the shallows," missing areas in which the potential for deeper insight abounds. To help you craft effective posts to address these two challenges, we've identified two classes of critical thinking strategies:

- Strategies that sharpen the focus of the dialogue
- Strategies that help participants dig deeper into the dialogue

For each general class, we've defined three substrategies targeting specific needs. As you can see in the figure below, *sharpening strategies* focus and constrain by making careful sense of an idea and clarifying it to create common ground. Ideas and directions are sorted out, and consensus on the direction of the dialogue is negotiated. *Digging-deeper* strategies can then build on common understandings, so that the participants reach for more generality or examine consequences. How can participants do this? By following inferences or exploring through analogies to get a wider feel for what's being said. Digging-deeper strategies, ultimately, shift the plane of the discussion as participants 1) embrace analogies or generalities that resonate, and 2) take on wider, more powerful and useful views of an idea.

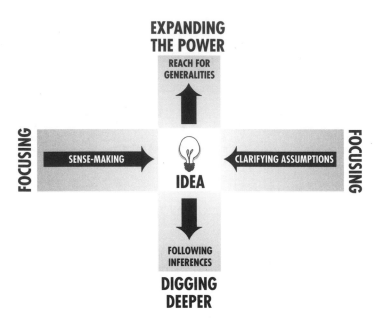

EXPANDING
THE POWER

REACH FOR
GENERALITIES

FOCUSING

SENSE-MAKING

IDEA

CLARIFYING ASSUMPTIONS

FOCUSING

FOLLOWING
INFERENCES

DIGGING
DEEPER

Dialogue-focusing strategies — such as *identifying direction, sorting ideas for relevance*, and *focusing on key points* — are handy if the dialogue loses direction, becomes too wordy, or becomes so dense that you simply must do some sorting or unpacking of ideas. Such "intellectual clean-up" — which involves putting things in order and making key issues prominent — is necessary in any dialogue.

Critical-thinking strategies that will help you and the discussion participants *dig deeper* include *full-spectrum questioning, making connections*, and *honoring multiple perspectives.* With these tools, you can add a deeper dimension to a dialogue that is "wallowing in the shallows" of a satisfactory, conventional approach or an unexamined vocabulary. You can also address critical issues of unexamined beliefs or assumptions that might block the path to productive thinking, or explore the reasons for these beliefs/disbeliefs through analogies, without arousing defensive reactions. By implementing digging-deeper strategies, then, you lay open for examination the rationale and implications of participants' contributions, and you move beyond advocacy of positions to consideration of the "why" aspect of propositions or claims that are held to be valid.

CRITICAL-THINKING STRATEGIES	
Sharpening the Focus	**Deepening the Dialogue**
Identifying Direction	Full-Spectrum Questioning
Sorting Ideas for Relevance	Making Connections
Focusing on Key Points	Honoring Multiple Perspectives

Let us now look more closely at the three *sharpening-the-focus* strategies. It's important to note that when you select any critical-thinking strategy, your intervention goal is not to instruct participants in critical thinking, or to reveal your own expertise. Instead, you must model the form and content of pragmatic dialogue, in which a "Guide on the Side" seeks to paraphrase, juxtapose, explore tensions or implications, or extend ideas to new levels of interpretation — all with the intent of finding new meaning. Ownership of the direction of the dialogue and the questions that drive it must remain with the participants.

SHARPENING THE FOCUS

Like face-to-face conversations or interactions in work groups or classrooms, online dialogues will often wander and lose their coherence. Thus, one of your central responsibilities as moderator is to maintain clarity of the discussion's direction and continually sharpen its focus. As such, you must assess the social and argumentative content of the online conversation and contribute — modeling pragmatic dialogue — entries designed to push the conversation forward. Negotiating the sense of space in the course or working group, and making clear its goals and expectations, is a process you must deal with continuously. Your role as concentrator of key contributions and keeper of coherence is essential in maintaining the direction of the dialogue (Bohm 1990).

You won't accomplish this task solely by marking out or moving toward rational ground. Rather, you'll succeed by carefully and collectively examining why a set of ideas or a position is incoherent. At both the start-up phase and within dialogues that are in full swing, sharpening-the-focus strategies are particularly useful (though they're not limited to these time frames). The start-up phase of any online dialogue brings awkward moments for participants and moderators alike. As we've noted previously, in online learning groups there is no "back rows of the work space or classroom" in which someone may invisibly "attend" the class. Everyone's contributions are written and public, and they require much more effort than head nods, smiles, or eye contact. As first entrant in a thread, you the moderator may wish to employ the voice of a Personal Muse and focus on key points or possible tensions, so that you can "break the ice" or provide some lines of discussion. Following some initial postings, you might next — now, perhaps, as a Conceptual Facilitator — highlight short, relevant segments from several lengthy responses, prizing gems of expression from a muddy matrix, to guide participants toward crisp language that supports the form of pragmatic dialogue. *Sharpening the focus* strategies inform participants informally of the standards and expectations of discourse, and they identify and highlight productive lines of discussion.

If, on the other hand, participants are fully engaged in a mature dialogue, focusing strategies may again come in handy. In mature dialogues, participants themselves may employ thinking strategies to dig for deeper meaning. As a Reflective Guide, you might bring to the surface intriguing, though ambiguous, ideas by citing key participant comments or even parts of assigned readings. Or, in the voice of a Mediator, you may want to cite different possible directions taken in the thread and negotiate paths in which the participants' collective energy can be best directed.

Let us now look at the three focusing-oriented critical-thinking strategies — *identifying direction, sorting ideas for relevance,* and *focusing on key points* — and study examples of their use in actual dialogues.

Identifying the Direction of a Dialogue

The first challenge you face as moderator is helping participants make sense of the general goals of an online working group or course, as well as the expectations of what it means to contribute to online dialogue. By carefully reflecting upon the entries in a thread, you can assess the general tack of the dialogue, its progress, and what appear to be digressions from the goals for each activity or discussion topic. Common concerns or interpretations give clues as to what participants see as worthwhile, noteworthy, or perhaps urgent. Digressions within individual communications and collective side trips can provide essential clues to participants' motivations or general lines of thinking. (They can also be unproductive sidebars best left without commentary.)

As the moderator wearing your Reflective Guide hat, you can select the *identifying-direction* strategy to sharpen the dialogue. You can refocus and perhaps redirect discussion to certain points or issues by selectively highlighting or paraphrasing pertinent lines of discourse. Similarly, as the voice of a Generative Guide, you can mull over potential meanings of phrases or topics and suggest possible directions and alternatives. Or, as a Conceptual Facilitator, you can weave and integrate ideas that may seem irrelevant on first reading but, when observed through another perspective, indicate valid and focused lines of thought.

In mature dialogues, you can use the voice of a Mediator and the identifying directions strategy to indicate current progress in the dialogue by highlighting tensions or unbalanced expositions. As a Conceptual Facilitator, you may elect to help identify direction by reviewing wording of assignments or key concepts for threads and citing participant usage, commentary, or possible turning points.

Example 7.1 Identifying Direction

Hands-on activities from *Craters!* (1995), a curriculum about craters on bodies in the solar system, were done at local sites. "Where was the inquiry in these activities?" was the assignment. Responses covered a wide range. The moderator sensed incoherence and tried to set out ways to pull the discussion together. The moderator elected to post a simple *identifying-direction* entry to collect ideas around a few strands of interest. The voice is that of a Conceptual Facilitator. The tone is neutral. (Note: The same excerpts are framed in a *making-connections* strategy in a later example to contrast the two types of strategies.)

What a busy time on the boards this week! The postings are numerous and all over the map.

On the **Do It Yourself Cratering** activity, some commented:

- "This activity supports the NSES Standard A — teaching with inquiry. The inquiry is the *doing* and just as important as the *discussing*."

The moderator begins with a social comment, then quickly shifts to six quotes from the discussion area. There are many tensions in the postings and a considerable amount of confusion about terms and expectations for inquiry.

- "This would be a very structured experience in inquiry. The teacher is a guide, a monitor, to keep them from going too far astray from the goal."

- "True, pure inquiry would be the way in which the original discoveries of our scientific laws were made, by the original scientists who discovered them. It took years before they knew that their theories were accurate."

- "The cratering activity was definitely an inquiry-based activity. We brainstormed the list of variables that existed in this activity — the list was incredible!"

- "The activities do not give the students the answers (relationships) they will discover. In that way, the activities are inquiry-based."

- "It is very structured and is not, in my opinion, inquiry. It is simply repeating a structured experiment."

The quotes highlight central ideas from posts that were often rather social. The moderator models the terse dialogue expected for pragmatic discourse.

Such variety! "Where is the inquiry in *Cratering?*" was the assignment. "In line with the standards," "definitely not inquiry at all," "very structured experience," "not like scientists do inquiry" are our answers. We don't all have to be on the same page here, at least at this early part of the course. Let's consider the common elements of the posts to see where our dialogue might be best directed.

The moderator decides not to pursue a common definition at this time, but to instead work toward clearer understanding of common terms.

Discussing or verbalizing seems central. Is it? And why?

Is inquiry more than "hands-on"? If so, how?

There seems to be a tension between inquiry and structure. Is it an opposition?

Discussion, "hands-on," and structure seem to need more precise formulation.

The moderator sets out options for direction.

Might "inquiry" be a label given to an activity at one time and with a certain population, and viewed as inaccurate for a different population or at a different time of year? What are the lines of discussion you want to pursue here?	*That "inquiry" may be a relational term is included in potential discussion threads.*

Sorting Ideas for Relevance

Any facilitator of online discussions reads, sorts, and rapidly assigns value to each discussion entry and its components based on the context of the topic or the course goals. The *sorting ideas for relevance* critical-thinking strategy addresses a very different process: Crafting an entry that explicitly, but informally, makes public the sorting mechanism, leaving options open for collective input.

In selecting this strategy, you the moderator make a conscious decision that the group needs to call attention to the sorting of ideas; all are not of equal weight. In a sorting for relevance post, you identify candidates for primary issues. You then identify the issues that might be tangents or digressions, and that, however appealing, the group should leave for another time. It's critical that you maintain in your posting indications of the participants' perceptions of relevance and direction. The sorting for relevance strategy focuses on relevance and importance; it differs sharply from a strategy intended to explore what direction the dialogue is taking. At issue is not what direction makes sense to pursue, but the relative importance of the active lines of thought.

In the start-up phase of a dialogue, sorting for relevance postings are often necessary. Like identifying direction postings, they help participants negotiate the sense of space and the expectations of their participation. As a Personal Muse using a sorting for relevance strategy, you may seek to model the process of online reflective dialogue by posing and responding to a sequence of directed questions that explore issues of relevance in concepts or the connections among ideas.

In mature dialogues, individual posts can become complex or lengthy, despite calls for concise expression. Individual posts, or perhaps a series of responses, often contain real gems trapped in murky or very diffuse prose. As such, you may wish to highlight these tidbits for the group by using a sorting for relevance strategy. Writing as a Conceptual Facilitator or perhaps in a Role Play, you can bring these nuggets to light and indicate the relative importance of lines of thought or concepts through narrative means. You may also seek to distinguish relevant and irrelevant issues by articulating, in crisp tales or metaphors, the directions discussions have taken to date.

Example 7.2 Sorting Ideas for Relevance

The following selection uses a *sorting for relevance* strategy in the voice of a Reflective Guide. The tone is neutral. The intervention came at a point in the dialogue when the participants had established the importance of assessment and students' personal involvement with material. However, the group members were still not clear about what they meant by assessment; nor were they clear on the purposes assessment served for themselves, their administrations, or their students.

MESSAGE SUBJECT: Are All Tools of Assessment Created Equal?

[Participant 1] asks about options beyond "the regular old quiz," or does that quiz "work just fine?"

[Participant 2] asks students, on a ten-question quiz, to make up two problems themselves and "solve them in whatever method is best for them." "I was amazed at what some of my students put down, and it really did give me a clear picture of where they were."

[Participant 3] sees himself more traditionally, and he cites a concern for making students "test ready." He wants to be sure kids can transfer knowledge from their experiences with manipulatives.

I suppose one needs to step back and sort out what we believe is the purpose and relevance of an assessment tool. We've got three very different takes on assessment here:

The entry starts without a social element — a moderator option. The dialogue is mature. The moderator pulls together important ideas and sorts out different meanings for assessment by comparing the three quotes.

- Does the type of assessment have to change when the learning experience changes?

- Testing what students think is a problem is as important as testing what they think is an answer. Does it make sense?

- Assessments should prepare students for the "real" assessments administered at local or state levels.

Are you interested in the answer, the process, and/or the progress of the student, or in the format of the question itself?

Are all modes of assessment created equal, and are they relevant in the pursuit of knowledge with regard to these areas? Which are the most relevant for you?

Each participant takes a very different tack on the use and importance of assessment. The moderator paraphrases, seeking to concentrate meaning on these different uses and concepts of assessment. The moderator highlights the tensions between traditional views and reform-minded or innovative approaches.

The moderator steps out of the dialogue and inquires about the "equality" of assessments, a purposely ambiguous term. How one would sort out issues is left to the respondents.

Focusing on Key Points

Though you may take the stance of a "Guide on the Side" in your moderating efforts, the process of moderating itself is essentially directive. *Focusing on key points*, as an online critical-thinking strategy, mirrors closely the function of highlighting key contributions — a tactic used by any skilled working group or classroom facilitator.

Using this approach, you the moderator work with participant input and draw on formal structures of the online experience, such as any specific goals for the group or conceptual organizers. The goal of your focusing on key points intervention: To highlight essential concepts and connections made to date. Your posting may also indicate potential omissions or areas of tension.

If you use a focusing on key points critical-thinking strategy in a post, it's important not to author your message with a view toward summarizing the dialogue or indicating where it might or should go. With this strategy, you simply paint a conceptual landscape of the terrain participants have visited and commented upon. The images and impressions are in the participants' words or phrasings, not yours. Leave assessments of completeness, value, or accuracy for your students to infer.

Whether it appears early or in more mature phases of a dialogue, a focusing on key points strategy is basically the same. In fact, focusing on key points is the only strategy that fits naturally with all six of the "voices" we described previously.

There are two central features of the focusing on key points strategy. The first is a list of ideas, citations, or contributions from the dialogue. The second is context for the list that articulates the connections or potential connections of the list elements and what these connections might mean.

If you become a Reflective Guide and use a focusing on key points strategy, you may want to highlight similar lines of thought in individual contributions or across multiple entries. As such, you might paraphrase or juxtapose comments or insights so that you can clarify or extend interaction with key points in the dialogue. If you employ a focusing on key points strategy as a Personal Muse, you can list, as part of a personal narrative, key issues or tensions raised within the discussion. You don't need to take a stand or attach any value to the entries or opinions cited.

The focusing on key points strategy will be crucial for you if you put on your Mediator hat. In this case, your posting must not only honor participants' positions or opposition, but also list and compare them, with an eye toward recognizing the common features in participants' reasons for holding assumptions or believing assertions.

A focusing on key points strategy will enable you as a Generative Guide to lay out existing contributions and indicate — by reference to goals or specific assignments, or perhaps to conceptual blocks that have developed — ways to approach potential areas or concepts that participants may have overlooked. Similarly, the focusing on key points strategy you might use in a Role Play could enumerate participants' contributions; an anecdote, a tale, or a character could sharpen perspectives on weakly articulated ideas or perhaps ideas that are missing altogether.

Example 7.3 Focusing on Key Points

This discussion on reform in science education is quite active. Familiar themes have emerged as central: Teachers' personal commitment, system or administrative support, and vision of potential practice. The moderator condenses three key issues in the dialogue, using a Conceptual Facilitator voice.

**MESSAGE SUBJECT:
What Supports Reform? Anything?**

[Participant 1] offers two thoughts on reform in science: "It's not all that hard in my current district to convince parents, colleagues, and administration that I'm covering the district core curriculum even though I don't follow it the way they intend. ... I've found that if they're well-enough informed, parents are more open to innovation than most schools give them credit for."

And ...

"Any top-down, widespread reform efforts I've seen have failed. I really think it's better to have a few interested teachers pilot new programs and let success speak for itself."

[Participant 2] shares her chat with a lady who did her thesis project on using inquiry and parent volunteers. The materials included "mini-labs for students to take home and use inquiry," involving parents by having "visits in science classes ... a few times a week." This study found "significant differences in the students' learning."

[Participant 3] notes: "We all can use improvement and change for the better; however, sometimes we are feeling like we need to change when maybe just a little augmenting is all we need ... in a different area. Again, I trust myself in

Again, the intervention starts without a social element. The title is crisp.

The first entry exudes self-confidence. Teachers here are seen as sources, implementers, and evaluators of reform.

The second entry is less certain. The participant cites anecdotally that there are other methods that are successful.

The last response sets its trust in personal experience. Small changes will bring people to success on the road of reform.

my decisions. There are so many decisions in the art of teaching."

Here we have three very different approaches:

- Confidence that bottom-up, teacher-piloted reform is what will work.
- Research in other peoples' classes shows that inquiry works. Parents can be helpers.
- Trust in one's own work and capacity to make minor course-correcting decisions is important.

The assignment inquired about your system and the value and support placed on reform. Do you have experiences that are different from those of [Participant 1], [Participant 2], and [Participant 3]?

The moderator places the quotes in the context of the main assignment, and invites others to contribute their thoughts and experiences.

Here's a second example of a focusing on key points strategy. In this case, the voice of a Reflective Guide lets the moderator explore the beliefs and motivations behind participants' comments:

Example 7.4 Focusing on Key Points

A very active discussion carried many lines of thought about what it means to teach with inquiry methods. The moderator selected several citations that contained themes of discomfort and crafted a post focusing attention on the idea of value and comfort and how these relate to the central assignment question, "What does it mean to do and teach with inquiry in algebra?" The tone is neutral. The quotes contain sufficient color and interest. The voice is that of a Reflective Guide commenting neutrally on tone and intent.

MESSAGE SUBJECT: An Uncomfortable Fit. Value and Comfort. [Participant 1], [Participant 2], [Participant 3], [Participant 4]

[Participant 1] expresses reservations about returning to a traditional setting:

"I don't know if my program could work in a traditional setting." She trusts her fellow elementary teachers, as they can "work with their students in similar ways — having multiple centers going on at one time." She muses: "When I return, I'll be taking my model with me to see if it works."

[Participant 2] sees some unexpected difficulties. "When I have used manipulatives, I've found the 'brighter' students complaining and even having difficulty with the tasks. They just wanted to move along and not spend time 'internalizing' concepts." He feels uneasy with this lack of attention: "They felt it was too elementary, and they also seemed to lack the patience."

[Participant 3] takes a philosopher's long view and notes that "in the end, students respond to your attitude. If you are satisfied with the results of conventional methods, they will sense that you are not sure there's a point to all the fuss about manipulatives or technology, or whatever." He seems to imply that students believe more than your words: "In such a situation, they are likely to resist."

There seems to be common ideas about valuing and comfort in these postings and in several others. Do these qualities always go together?

[Participant 4] writes openly about our own mediocrity: "Maybe we need to quit saying we don't change because of tests, and admit that we don't change because we're not comfortable trying new things. Mediocrity that we're used to is easier to accept in ourselves than the new threat of failure."

The moderator begins with direct citations. She bolds names and includes them in the title to honor contributions. She condenses the quotes from a longer narrative and social context. The dialogue is mature; digging deeper strategies are unnecessary.

Personal doubts, even criticism, show up in [Participant 4]'s note. Its language is quite crisp, and it provides sufficient tension and the potential for disagreement. The moderator places it last, as the type of personal reflection on the meaning of inquiry for a practitioner is particularly relevant.

[Participant 1], [Participant 2], and [Participant 3] comment on professional feelings of uncertainty and surprise regarding the use of inquiry.

Teaching with inquiry brings some burdens, as these responses are telling us. Being uncomfortable and open to failure may be a characteristic of inquiry learning and teaching. Is it?

These changes, and inquiry learning itself, seem to be like walking with ill-fitting shoes. Does this mean we must find ways to help ourselves and our students be comfortable with irritation?

The posting concludes with a metaphor — "ill-fitting shoes" — for the discomfort one might feel using inquiry and approaching change.

DEEPENING THE DIALOGUE

Maintaining forward momentum in a dialogue requires more than sharpening the discussion's focus and keeping important ideas in the forefront. Dialogues progress because participants feel there are areas they haven't explored and ideas whose implications and connections they need to follow.

In some dialogues, participants naturally follow conceptual trails into the unknown. In others, however, you the facilitator must help the participants become aware of unseen potential. We've identified three critical-thinking strategies that help push dialogue to new areas. These strategies explore or highlight existing tensions or conceptual blocks, challenge or identify assumptions or barriers to new conceptualizations, or approach issues from multiple angles. The strategies are:

- Full-spectrum questioning
- Making connections
- Honoring multiple perspectives

You can use these strategies in either the start-up phase of discussions or within the interactions of mature dialogues, but they are of particular importance in the transition phase. In that phase, participants have some idea of the expectations of online contribution, and they've gone beyond social or argumentative formats to a basic use of pragmatic dialogue. However, they're not yet aware of how sharing reflections publicly online can bring new perspectives and depth to their own thinking. As moderator, using these *digging-deeper* strategies, you can help participants value reflections and uncertainty as bridges to new levels in their own thoughts and examinations of their personal beliefs and assumptions.

Critical thinking strategies can readily generate questions. But, one must ask, "Are questions the main tools available to facilitate dialogue?" Questions, we have found, are but *one* of the tools available. Moderation techniques focusing on the production or honing of questioning skills run the risk of wresting ownership of the dialogue from its contributors. So as the "Guide on the Side," you must also avail yourself of techniques that explore tensions without seeking resolution, examine rationale for beliefs or assumptions without assigning value, and interpret at different levels while leaving to the participants the formulation of the driving questions that push a dialogue deeper.

By paying close attention to this type of interaction — deepening the dialogue by going beyond question formulation to the context and beliefs/assumptions behind people's assertions — you can model and encourage the kind of thinking and ownership of new ideas necessary to push dialogue deeper.

Let us now look closely at the three specific strategies you can use to deepen the dialogue in online discussions. We begin with *full-spectrum questioning*.

Full-Spectrum Questioning

Who? What? When? Where? Why? We're all familiar with the questioning strategies employed by journalistic or expository writing. The purpose of questioning in such a context is to gather sufficient information so that a writer can inform the reader of some event or process. A reader of journalistic or expository prose, likewise, seeks out these signposts as indicators of what's being conveyed in the article.

But in a pragmatic dialogue, as we have defined the term, questions and questioning strategies serve a very different purpose. There is no story to get out, nor are there signposts, in any traditional sense, indicating what the reader might expect the prose to say. In fact, questions that help you facilitate pragmatic dialogue have an instrumental value that goes far beyond delivering or even clarifying facts. As moderator, you can post question-based interventions to help the participants examine their own hypotheses, thoughts, and beliefs, both individually and collectively.

The "five w's" above elicit answers to be sure. But, however complete or informative those answers might be, they don't adequately serve the needs of an online learning community. That's why we offer you the *full-spectrum questioning* techniques described below, which can serve as a sort of scaffold for you as you seek ways to frame questions in a reflective dialogue.

If you're like most facilitators and participants, you've had little experience or training in the models of questioning that go beyond the "five w's." As such, you'll likely bring to your facilitation efforts a highly limited set of tools to explore your own thinking and that of others. And the difficulties can compound for you if you attempt to bring inquiry into your dialogue, since your skill in formulating questions can compete with participants' seeking to direct their own learning.

That's why we've adapted to the online setting some guidelines for questioning strategies in face-to-face group work devised by Dennis Matthies (1996), Matthew Lippman (1991), and others in the critical-thinking movement. The method presented here, called *full-spectrum questioning,* has been adapted from Matthies's strategies for face-to-face meetings. Compared with the "five w's" of journalism, this approach offers you the moderator a much wider palette to frame and conceive questions based on participant responses.

Our treatment of full-spectrum questioning is more detailed than that we afford to other critical-thinking techniques because the material represents a synthesis of approaches not described in current literature on online dialogue.

To the right is a table exploring all five levels of full-spectrum questioning:

Full-spectrum questioning offers five general categories of questions, with each category designed to extract layers of meaning when applied to words, processes, statements, or directions of a dialogue. By modeling these richer modes of questioning, you can help participants find new ways of viewing and questioning their own thinking.

The five categories of full-spectrum questioning are:

- "So what?" questions
- Questions that clarify meaning
- Questions that explore assumptions and sources
- Questions that identify cause and effect
- Questions that plan a course of action

FULL-SPECTRUM QUESTIONING

Questions that probe the "so what!" response	Questions that clarify meaning or conceptual vocabulary	Questions that explore assumptions, sources, and rationale	Questions that seek to identify causes and effects or outcomes	Questions that consider appropriate action
How Relevant or Important? To whom? To what constituency? Individuals or groups? What viewpoint would impart importance? Is that me/us/them? What audience is assumed? If we knew all about this, what good would it do? **How Urgent or Interesting?** Is immediate consideration needed? Or, is the detail best left for other times or forums? Is the issue compelling, or tangentially related to my or the group's task at hand? Is the issue of intellectual merit? **What Context?** Is the issue or question part of a larger view or strategy?	**Is there Ambiguity or Vagueness?** Are terms clear or meanings commonly shared? What alternative meanings might exist? Can quantifiers be made more explicit? How much? How long? How few? To what extent? Can implicit comparisons be made explicit? **Are Concepts Held in Common?** Are terms relying on professional or technical understandings? Does meaning shift from ordinary usage to technical sense? Is persuasion confused with definition? What might be a similar example in another area?	**What Qualities Are Assumed?** Is the claim or phenomena assumed to be: Real, unique, measurable, beneficial, harmful, neutral? Might the opposite assumption be equally valid? Are biases or preconceptions evident in gender, audience, categorization? What does the speaker assume about herself or himself or the audience? **Can One Be Sure?** What evidence supports the claim? How can it be confirmed? What are reasons for belief or disbelief or assigning value? What procedures or processes give evidence for certainty? What supports any analogies?	**Primary vs. Secondary?** Is the claim/condition a root or secondary cause or effect? Is it a trigger for other mechanisms? What are they? **Internal/External vs. Systematic Interaction** Is the cause/effect mechanism internal or partly external to the system? What external factors affect interactions? Are reputed "causes" perhaps correlations? At what level might true causes operate? Are consequences long or short term? For whom? What limits or scenarios might apply? What are worst/best cases? What is most probable? Why? If cause/effects are connected systemically through feedback, what are the key feedback controls?	**Who Does What, How, When, with Whom, and Why?** Is there a quick fix or is a more considered view needed? Should I/we do something? Together, separately, as a group? Should it be done now? When? What is the commitment? Are those involved too close to act effectively? Are outsiders needed? Who can be engaged? What plans or strategies will be effective? What levels/conditions need addressing first? **What Comes Next?** How is effectiveness evaluated? What ongoing monitoring or re-evaluating of intervention is needed? Is there a backup plan? Who directs it? Under what conditions is it operative?

Full-spectrum questioning is not a taxonomy or even a hierarchy of levels of questions for you to work through in a specific sequence. Rather, it presents — like an artist's palette — a more varied, more subtle range of options and potential effects that you can obtain as you pose questions in online discussions.

You may employ full-spectrum questioning at any phase of a dialogue. However, we suggest two main categories of use: "sweeping the decks" and "levering out of a rut."

In online communities, as in their face-to-face counterparts, participants often assume common understanding of terms, or common assumptions about causes or the need for action. The "building community" aspect of any course encourages such thinking. Thus, dialogue in the initial phases of online discussion can proceed along diffuse, or even muddy, lines of thinking. "Sweeping the decks" by seeking to clarify terms, by teasing apart ideas, or by reframing poorly formed or implicit questions is one way you can effectively use full-spectrum questioning. By "cleaning up" the ground work, you can lay the sound content foundation that is essential for dialogue to proceed meaningfully. How can you do this? Perhaps as the voice of a Personal Muse, you can employ full-spectrum questioning to explore questions before the group and grapple with direction, ambiguity, or possible assumptions. Or perhaps, as a Mediator, you could paraphrase questions or issues and seek commonality at a higher level by resolving ambiguities or misunderstood assumptions or beliefs.

You can also use full-spectrum questioning to guide participants out of a situation that is common in professional dialogues: Conversations confined by a common terminology or set of standard approaches that blocks off paths to new ways of thinking and seeing. We call this full-spectrum questioning strategy "levering out of a rut." Issues relating to the validity and certainty of particular sources, helpfulness, and the identification of cause and effect may need highlighting and examination from completely different perspectives. As moderator, then, you might ask: "How do we know _____ is true, accurate, measurable, or even beneficial, or that the effect assumed is real or not?" The voice of a Generative Guide or Conceptual Facilitator is well suited to this task of breaking the mold of convention to consider ideas in a new light.

A note of caution is necessary when it comes to using full-spectrum questioning in online dialogue. Full-spectrum questioning is only one of a much wider set of tools for moderation. It is structured, relatively easy to apply, but content-neutral. It focuses on questions themselves. But a question is by no means the only tool you can or should use to encourage inquiry. Questions, particularly good ones, command attention. Thus, overusing a technique like full-spectrum questioning carries potential risks. Among them: competing with participants for ownership of the dialogue's direction; and overly appreciating questions themselves — and not participants' grappling with them — as centerpieces of the dialogue.

Let us now briefly examine the five categories of full-spectrum questioning, beginning with those focusing on the concept of "so what?"

Questions that probe the "so what?" response. Any issue or concern must first pass a threshold of critical relevance and urgency before there is any further dialogue upon it. The "so what?" questions you ask may appear curt or overly pointed, but in a pragmatic dialogue they're essential in identifying interest, context, relevance, and urgency within a limited time frame. Thus, you should include a question like, "Why do we really need to consider this issue?" — at least by implication — in the beginning of any interaction.

Relevance or importance is one outlook you can address with the "so what?" question: "To whom is this concern of interest or relevance?" "To what constituency is it addressed?" "Is it keyed to individuals or groups?" "Is that me/us/them?" "What audience is assumed for any response?" "Were we to know all about this topic, what good would it do?" As facilitator, you may want to echo or highlight explicit or implicit tensions in initial responses to these types of questions to help the participants clarify the direction of the dialogue.

Urgency or interest is another outlook you must probe before you and the participants commit your time and resources to a particular discussion: "Is immediate consideration needed? Or is the detail best left for other times or forums?" "Is the issue compelling, or is it only tangentially related to my/the group's task at hand?" "Is this an issue of intellectual merit?"

Questions that clarify meaning or conceptual vocabulary. Ambiguity and vagueness are important features to either clarify or to use in sustaining the tension that supports dialogue. As moderator, you may see wandering conversations emerge from participants' unclear use of terms or from presumed common meanings. A posting from you in such a situation can explore alternative meanings that might exist, or perhaps look at how quantifiers or comparisons can be made more explicit.

By quoting or paraphrasing participants' responses, you can also highlight or hold up for commentary concepts, professional or technical understandings, or usages that may or may not be held in common among the participants. Differences between ordinary language usage and narrow technical applications may sustain confusion. As moderator, you can bring to the surface for examination and reflection several different meanings used by the participants.

It's important, however, not to appear to be a quibbler or stickler who is demanding and appreciative of precise phrasing. The intent of the usage or definition is central to the illuminating task of moderation. Is the author of a message building new meanings for terms in light of a specific conceptual framework? Or are new meanings being coined using metaphors or extending existing constructs? Or is the author attempting to influence opinion under the guise of crafting a definition in a rhetorical attempt to persuade? By singling out various meaning-making attempts using the voice of a Personal Muse, a Reflective or Generative Guide, or even a Conceptual Facilitator, you can help the group members look more deeply at their own thinking and its implications.

Questions that explore assumptions, sources, and rationale. Participants' entries, both as social dialogue and as contributions to pragmatic discussions, reveal a great deal about the writers' qualities, assumptions, and beliefs. As part of your "sweeping the decks" role, you can explore alternative meanings or possible tensions based on assumptions conveyed in the words of the participants. You could, for example, openly muse about certain assertions, asking if the group has really thought about whether a claim or phenomena is real, unique, measurable, beneficial, harmful, or neutral.

In an effort to "lever a group out of a rut," you might, for instance, suggest that participants consider whether the opposite assumption to a commonly held belief might be equally valid. You could also ask the participants to consider any biases or preconceptions that might be evident in their thinking based on gender, audience, or categorization.

As a Generative Guide, you could suggest that participants think about evidence for their claims, or about their reasons for belief, disbelief, or assigning value. As a Conceptual Facilitator, you might direct the discussion to help participants ponder the concept of certainty. And as a Mediator, you could attempt to extend participants' thinking with analogies by examining the bases of those offered or seeking new ones emphasizing common goals.

Internal/external vs. systemic interaction. Issues that relate to identifying cause and effect are commonly problematic in online discussions. Participants can confuse the dialogue by neglecting to articulate to the group, or perhaps even to themselves, the assumptions or connections inherent in their viewpoints as either internal or partly external to their conceptual frames. In a clarifying role, you can intervene in this type of situation with paraphrases of people's positions. You can also highlight external factors, reputed causes or correlations, and suggestions on the levels upon which true causes may operate.

To move dialogue beyond well-trodden paths in a discussion in which interpretations or positions may have begun to solidify, you can suggest that participants consider both long- and short-term consequences for each position, as individuals and for the group or associated parties. Perhaps you can highlight best- and worst-case scenarios, or the limits of participants' frames or interpretations, to indicate the wide range of thinking among the participants. If stale thinking is evident, there is very possibly some feedback or assumptions maintaining it. As moderator, you can analyze conversations to look for patterns, so that you can in turn find rules or assumptions that are limiting the dialogue. You can also hold these rules or assumptions up for discussion.

Just as unrecognized assumptions or interactions in physical or fiscal systems can either determine or support repeated unfavorable results, unrecognized feedback loops can also be present in social interactions and can lie at the foundation of recurrent roadblocks or conceptual impasses. As moderator, you can post a message that questions or invites examination of key assumptions or conceptual links that participants see as central to the problems.

Questions that consider appropriate action. If an idea is attractive or a cause seems worthy, a common first step is to consider, "What shall we do now to fix it or help out?" Discussants tend to forge ahead right away, assuming common ground and without first "sweeping the decks" to figure out if there really is agreement about what's being talked about, or without taking time to question agreed-upon value assumptions behind particular assertions.

By inviting participants to more thoughtfully consider an issue and the potential problems it might entail, you can bring into question the notion that there is a "quick fix" or "something we should do now." As facilitator using the voice of a Generative Guide or Mediator, you can highlight questions or excitements stemming from the "so what?" category so that they're juxtaposed with a more detailed examination of their appropriateness: "Are we the ones who should be acting here? Do we work individually or in concert? Are outsiders better choices? And what is the commitment assumed?" Exploring terms and assumptions can bring together an excited but loosely focused dialogue, encouraging participants to reconsider issues related to action.

Discussants who are "stuck in a rut" are not always in static condition. The "rut" can be a direction or an attraction the group can't resist, but which they still can't get to for any number of reasons. As the moderator diagnosing such a condition, you can intervene. Citing or paraphrasing participants' entries, you can question how plans or strategies will be considered effective, or which conditions need to be addressed in sequence. If participants commonly assume that a certain direction is productive or healthy, you can — through Role Plays or as a Personal Muse — wonder "aloud" about monitoring, re-evaluating, or the existence or usefulness of a backup strategy.

The following example illustrates how a moderator might step in when group members have gotten "carried away" on an issue, leaving pragmatic dialogue in the dust as they enthusiastically trade comments about how administrators might become closer in touch with the realities of classroom teaching. This moderator uses full-spectrum questioning to help the group slow down, take a breath, and do a bit of a "reality check" of its own. The moderator uses humor to bring the group down gently, albeit firmly:

Example 7.5 Full-Spectrum Questioning

Here's a model of how you might use *full-spectrum questioning* in your moderating efforts. In a reading, the phrase "principal sharing the same foxhole" captured participants' attention but not their imaginations. The dialogue had circled endlessly about well-trodden paths. New ways to look at the idea seemed out of reach. This post employs a Generative Guide voice using the framework of *full-spectrum questioning* to look at new avenues of thought. The tone of the entry is humorous, the result provocative.

MESSAGE SUBJECT: "In the Same Foxhole." What Does This Mean?

There have been many contributions to this thread on how administrators can support reform in education. We all seem to be charmed by that phrase "in the same foxhole." "In the same foxhole" sounds neat, but what meaning have we agreed upon? [Participant 1], [Participant 2], and [Participant 3] seem to understand it as an administrator coming to their classroom to share experiences, perhaps co-teach, or even take over some classroom duties. [Participant 4], [Participant 5], [Participant 6], and [Participant 7] seem to feel that "in the same foxhole" means some type of mutual experience of the same kinds of frustrations, "to be like us."

How much sharing of foxholes are we talking about during one year? One hour, one day, a week? Even if administrators do come in, what really is shared? Certainly there is potential for shared confusion over what is to be taught and how.

We seem to assume that being "in the same foxhole" is a good thing. Let's assume the war metaphor has some value for the moment. Isn't it possible that a well-intentioned principal

The title challenges the meaning of the attractive phrase.

The moderator sets out paraphrases and short citations from seven respondents. She makes two general groupings, based on the participants' interpretations of what is good about being "in the same foxhole." The moderator also points out that there seems to be no common meaning of the phrase.

dropping into some foxholes in his school might be shot by mutinous troops? At the minimum, such coziness may invite long visits by a union steward. "Foxhole sharing is a form of non-contractual evaluation," the union says.

Is there a causal connection between being "in the foxhole" and principals being better administrators? A principal can be an excellent, mediocre, or poor teacher. So what? Their content training may be inappropriate, and even if it's not it may be outdated. There are consequences of the time spent out of her foxhole and in yours that need to be considered.

Even if foxhole sharing does offer all sorts of information and feedback, what are both sides going to do with it? Is there a short- and long-term plan for processing the experience?

Can some of these considerations inform us about what is so attractive about the "sharing a foxhole" idea? The group values this sharing. But what is it about the idea, in a practical sense, that resonates with helping teachers do their jobs better?

Using full-spectrum questioning, the moderator sets out to widen perspectives. She challenges the value of the "foxhole" phrase. Is it good? She then invites quantification of the foxhole "sharing." She identifies potential problems by using a humorous scenario. Using ideas from the categories of full-spectrum questioning, she explores causal connections

Even if the physical "foxhole" sharing happens, the moderator asks about what's to be done with the experience.

The post ends with a request for deeper thinking about "sharing." What can this mean for a team of teachers and administrators?

You need not use the full-spectrum questioning strategy solely to generate questions. The strategy's classes of questions can guide you in creating a composition that attempts to explore in one narrative many sides of an issue. Think of such a post as a tentative response to a set of full-spectrum questions posed by a Personal Muse.

Example 7.6 Full-Spectrum Questioning

In the following post, crafted using *full-spectrum questioning,* the moderator attempts to engage a group that has been "wallowing in the shallows" about the use of projects and highly engaging activities. A vision of what project work might look like in a classroom has not quite gelled. How does project work personally engage students on lines that support the curriculum? The moderator employs a Personal Muse voice in a narrative style, along with a full-spectrum questioning strategy that lays out all sorts of options for approaching curricular decisions. The moderator also describes what effects these decisions might have. Tentative responses to questions from each of the categories of full-spectrum questioning are central to the posting. The post invites commentary.

MESSAGE SUBJECT:
Standardized Tests/Inquiry,
Outcomes, Messing Around

It has been interesting in my honors physics classes this past month. I gave my students a long-term research project, wherein groups of students had to choose a project that would result in a tangible product — build something and then carry out original research with that object. The "Amateur Scientist" column in *Scientific American* contains many ideas on this topic. One girl is grinding the mirror for her eight-inch reflecting telescope. Another group is building a haze photometer and hopes to contribute data to the national data bank. Others are building a wind tunnel, a Ramsden machine, or analyzing the motion of a runner.

The message subject links three threads that had significant discussion. A social introduction sets a context — a classroom not unlike those of the participants.

The narrative, in the voice of a teacher/ moderator, captures the main assignment and the efforts of several student projects. The moderator explores what a project might mean. He describes mid-course corrections and goal shifts. Students have different meanings for "doing a project."

The kids got the assignment right after Christmas. Once a week or so, I gave some class time to do research or to work on their project. Everything was sputtering along. Mid-April was my time frame for an exhibition of projects. In my mind, by early March, the constructing part would be done

The moderator muses on his expectations and schedules as they're adjusted. He approaches effects of the new meaning for doing projects, leaving the exact time commitment ambiguous.

and the research part would be in full swing. In reality, wheels spun for two months.

So I had to punt. I told students that they could bring in their projects and then do the construction in my classroom. At least that way I could monitor progress and provide periodic momentum boosts. (I can also see my content fly out the window — whoops, did I lose diffraction? ...)

The moderator reflects on the value of the projects and the initial failure.

Slowly, the projects are taking shape. What I forget is how important false starts are. It is one thing to run a lab for two days; it is quite another to see something take shape and to have to form it as you go along. A month ago, [Student 1's] mirror focused at infinity. Yesterday, it focused at 50 inches, almost to her 48-inch goal. The rough grind is over, and now the finer grinding begins. I have spent so much time watching in frustration as I saw kids waste the time I gave them in class, but now I also see thoughtful products being assembled. I can almost see the thoughts of the kids as they try one thing after another before the right solution comes along.

The moderator gives examples of student work. He also questions and gives a partial resolution to the frustrations of devoting considerable time to project work. He muses that projects and their processes leave a visible trail of thought. What is the value of such evidence?

I'm still real nervous. What if the senior slide hits and nothing is done with these fantastic products? What if the wind tunnel never sails? What if the video of the runner never gets clearly resolved? My curriculum is like my student's telescope: Noisy, sometimes screechy, very rough, yet I have to start somewhere.

In closing, the moderator uses a metaphor to capture the similarities between projects and the process of teaching. He leaves open issues relating to response to testing.

I think I started this post as a comment on inquiry and testing. I have no idea how this last month gets put into a standardized test. I think it has to fit into another assessment.

Making Connections

Barriers to deeper thinking can take on many forms. Two general barriers can be characterized as either internal to the ideas or concepts themselves, or internal to the individuals working with those ideas or concepts. Some ideas or concepts contain links or even essential similarities that can remain obscure to participants unless you the moderator expend effort stretching the participants' imaginations or conceptual frames. Using tensions, metaphors, or unusual juxtapositions, you can turn participants' conventional understandings or interpretations into more general ones.

Participants can also hold assumptions or beliefs that block, or make difficult, connections in different contexts or at deeper levels. A *making-connections* strategy on your part can move the dialogue beyond these barriers.

"Making connections," used in this sense, goes far beyond amplifying an idea by finding multiple examples at the same level or in a similar context; such connections are merely associative, and you can address them by using focusing strategies that clarify meaning. A making-connections strategy challenges participants to go beyond "more of the same" to explore, at an individual and a group level, inferences, tensions, and perhaps rationales for statements in the discussion, and to move beyond first-look interpretations. Using the making-connections strategy, you attempt to help participants make shifts to deeper layers of meaning in their communications.

You may also seek to explore patterns of beliefs and assumptions by modeling the willing suspension of belief. One method for doing this is questioning the value of a widely held assumption or offering a support-ive commentary that interprets statements from an unusual view. Your goal in this case is to move individuals and the group beyond a stance of advo-cating personal or collective visions, and toward an open consideration of why they hold their beliefs and see their assumptions as valid.

Making connections differs from full-spectrum questioning in two respects. The goal of a making connections posting is not to set out a suite of intrigu-ing questions, nor is it to explore any particular question type. A making-connections post may not contain a question posed by you at all; instead, the best approach might feature a simple commentary or a tale containing alternative interpretations. The purpose of the making-connections strategy is to shift the level of discussion, and then let participants take it from there. It pushes participants to higher levels of thinking so that they can examine inferences or explore beliefs or assumptions openly. Thus, the tools of the making-connections posting are analogy, inference, and modeling the suspension of advocacy in the spirit of inquiry.

Using the making-connections approach with a Personal Muse or Role Play voice, you might offer a comical tale or an anecdote to model the suspension of judgments, beliefs, or disbeliefs as potential blocks to seeing a bigger picture. Using the voice of a Generative Guide, you can offer new interpretations or options that seek to expose barriers to inquiry that lie in participants' belief systems or assumptions. A Personal Muse entry in this context can also highlight the tensions between advocacy and inquiry, and point out the potential barriers to searching for solutions.

Making-connections postings are particularly effective in the middle phase of dialogue, when the negotiation of the space and expectations comes to a close. By using this strategy, you model for the participants' interaction through pragmatic dialogue, and the advances to be gained by moving to a different way of approaching beliefs and assumptions.

Example 7.7 Making Connections

The group had been "wallowing in the shallows" and was not quite engaged in what it means to go beyond their own positions to examine reasons for making statements and examining their own assumptions. The critical-thinking strategy of *making connections,* using a Personal Muse voice and a powerful metaphor, provides a way to look at alternatives out in the open without directly challenging participants' positions.

MESSAGE SUBJECT:
Looking Around

The faculty and department meetings are in full swing. Attendance, discipline, schedules, meeting the (totally unspecified) standards, delayed books and supplies ... I confess to letting my mind wander. At one point I looked out the window and spaced a bit, needing some

The moderator starts with a scene-setting paragraph — a musing out the window. Thoughts from the netcourse dialogue appear, appeal, and clash.

interaction with the real challenges of teaching. Four thoughts from the course dialogue echoed in my mind.

I could agree with each one, even though some might seem contradictory! But something wasn't gelling … an image about gardening and onions from the course introduction flashed into my mind. A novice gardener asks: "How do I grow bigger flowers on my onions?" For him, the purpose of the gardening is out of focus. He is intrigued by the wrong end of the plant; onions are grown to eat, not to admire their blooms! Where am I perhaps led astray by focusing on the wrong end of the "inquiry onion"?

Putting myself in the role of the master "gardener of inquiry," I tried looking at the comments to see what made them stay with me, and perhaps what misleads — the focus being on the wrong end of the onion:

"Inquiry is the doing and, just as important, the discussing." Had I put much importance on doing? Can the signs of good inquiry be pauses in dialogues — doing nothing? How might I know inquiry is going on?

"The teacher is a guide, a monitor, to keep students from going too far

The imaginative tone and Personal Muse voice, combined with a visual metaphor, permit the moderator to examine areas she could not approach directly without fear of criticism or confrontation.

The moderator models reflection on one's own beliefs and assumptions. She acknowledges the fact that a person can support and deem reasonable contradictory statements.

The moderator turns each of the participants' quotes inward to explore, "Yes, I believe this, but why?"

astray. ..." Teacher as guide/monitor/shepherd is not new; we've all done our share of sheepherding. What about the "guide" process supports inquiry — or might my guiding, nurturing efforts interfere?

"True, pure inquiry would be the way in which the original discoveries of our scientific laws were made, by the original scientists who discovered them." That thrill of discovery must have been great, but is "true inquiry" only for original scientists? Does trying to emulate the great names and lauding their achievements keep others from their own inquiry? Does (did?) it keep me and my students from owning our own learning?

The moderator sets out alternative interpretations to the four statements. But she doesn't criticize them as incorrect or inaccurate.

"It is very structured and is not, in my opinion, inquiry. It is simply repeating a structured experiment." The back of my mind echoed, "Can the neat inquiry labs I wrote up this year be replayed for next year's class? Am I trying to carve inquiry labs into structured experiments? How much serendipity is assumed doing inquiry?"

The post invites participants to consider alternative beliefs to their postings. The moderator encourages participants to share ideas that something might be seemingly intelligent, even necessary, but, from experience, block the doing of math or science.

Looking from the other side — away from the "flowers" that attract us — can you see other seemingly intelligent assumptions or beliefs that may block the path to doing science or math?

[Moderator]

Making connections is an important strategy because it gives you the means to move, from one plane to another, a dialogue that is trapped in terminology or expectations.

Another example:

Example 7.8 Making Connections

Though the dialogue has been quite active, beliefs and assumptions behind statements have not been well articulated. The participants have worked with inquiry and manipulative methods in algebra for two months, but they still seem to treat it externally, like a foreign language that has to be translated into traditional procedures to be understood. Using a Role Play centered on a personal anecdote, and a Conceptual Facilitator voice, the moderator attempts to help participants view algebra through different eyes.

MESSAGE SUBJECT:
Blinded by Vision

[Participant 1] asks, "Even if we do get an understanding of operations with blocks, will it translate back to symbolic operations on paper?"

The moderator presents three comments on the use of manipulatives in learning and teaching algebra.

[Participant 2] wonders how students "can understand the use of manipulatives in algebra. Isn't it an added burden? I have to translate this into algebraic notation to understand it at all. ... My bright students just want to memorize the steps to get to the answer."

The moderator clearly sets out issues of differences between the use of manipulatives and symbolic representation of algebraic expressions and the use of algorithms.

[Participant 3] comments that "her very bright, college-age daughter tried the manipulatives and was confused by them." She questions their use with "weaker students who are confused already."

Translating from one world view to another seems to be a common concern. I'd like to share one of those "unexpected translations" I had with a blind student in my algebra class. [Student] really challenged what I thought was my strength — my "visual" teaching style. I thought I could show students anything clearly. Well, everything had to be carefully redesigned.

The moderator brings up a narrative from her own experience. She remarks on her visual style and the changes she had to make to accommodate a blind student. Equity in mathematics education is imminent in the response, but not directly touched upon.

We managed quite well until we got to multiplication of polynomials. I usually teach this from a trial-and-error approach — requiring vision. We used Algeblocks (algebra manipulatives) with [Student]. I taught him to represent quadratic polynomials by multiplying, say, x+2 on one side, x+1 on the other, to get a rectangle made of $x^2 + 2x + x + 2$. He experienced trial and error to make the rectangle.

When asked to do a factoring demo for the group, [Student] showed, with the blocks, that factoring was quite literally the reverse process. He used blocks to construct a rectangle, from blocks like $x^2 + 3x + 2$. Then he identified the sides to find the factors. If one had +3 instead of +2, anybody shuffling around the blocks gets a rectangle, side (z+1) other side (z+2) but one block. $z^2 + 3z + 3$ is prime! Never thought of it this way! I had to keep on my toes here!

[Student's] methods show the teacher a new way of thinking. Prime numbers can't be made into rectangles with blocks. Neither can prime polynomials. The moderator, a teacher herself, lays herself open to new knowledge.

I thought, at first, that this was a unique perspective. I'd always done factoring symbolically. But [Student] quite easily "saw" that factoring and multiplication were related, just like division and multiplication of integers. I still wonder about the concrete visualizations [Student] made, which he could see but I could not.

Left unresolved is the issue of what is meant by "seeing" algebra or algebraic expressions.

[Student] brought me into a new world of seeing algebra.

Does anyone else have similar "aha!" moments to share in algebra or any other area? Does our training, even our expertise, separate us, as much as it helps us, from understanding students' problems and ways of working through them?

The moderator invites participants to move outside their own reference frames and recount the "seeing" of algebra differently.

Honoring multiple perspectives. To most topics, including educational ones, people often bring a fixed, or even hardened, perspective. The reasons for this calcification are many, and beyond the scope of this book. But getting beyond the baggage of specific positions and focusing on common goals is central to the process of nurturing dialogue and bringing about understanding in online discussions.

Honoring multiple perspectives differs from other "digging-deeper" strategies in that it builds upon the layers of understanding attained through applying the techniques of making connections and full-spectrum questioning. In general, you use the honoring-multiple-perspectives approach in mature dialogues, in which the participants are comfortable with detaching themselves from particular beliefs or assumptions and are amenable to considering widely differing viewpoints. The multiple-perspectives technique is commonly the last step before a working group, assigned the task of evaluating and recommending particular programs, completes its process. Such a conclusion represents a collective decision and a statement of advocacy, achieved after the inquiry process has revealed all viable options.

Without favoring any particular viewpoint, you the moderator can use the honoring multiple perspectives approach as a Conceptual Facilitator to introduce or validate multiple perspectives on key issues. Your intention should not be to summarize, but to simply lay out a landscape of views.

As a Mediator, you might want to honor multiple perspectives while seeking service to common goals. Or, as a Generative Guide, you may seek to model alternatives to confined thinking by incorporating multiple perspectives as springboards to alternative interpretations.

Example 7.9 Honoring Multiple Perspectives

In the following example, the moderator uses the *honoring-multiple-perspectives* strategy to encourage deeper reflection on an exercise in INTEC. The exercise involved inviting students to take web-based conceptual probes on science and math concepts. Responses were anonymous. Questions in the probe were slightly unformed, inviting interpretation by the respondents. Their interpretations revealed their level of understanding. Participants were asked to view summaries of data, displayed anonymously, and to find patterns and comment. The voice

---

here is that of a Conceptual Facilitator. There is tension in the entries. Mediation is not necessary, as it isn't important for this activity. That all respondents be in agreement on what's said is not foremost. In this particular case, the blasé response is as significant — perhaps more so — as the teacher being troubled by what her students demonstrated. Can a deeper understanding of the rationale behind others' responses be reached? The tone is neutral.

MESSAGE SUBJECT: Probe Data: Gold Mine or Slag Heap?

Participants report that students' responses in the Conceptual Probes Summary page show intriguing patterns. Many different or opposing interpretations have emerged in our discussion.

[Participant 1] is quite certain that the results show nothing. The questions are slightly unfocused by design. He thinks they "confuse students who approach them. Little can be said about what students really know using poorly worded questions."

[Participant 2] says, "I'm horrified. Many talented students made errors they just should not have made. Few got any fully correct." She notes that she had never appreciated the power of the misconceptions the students bring to the class.

"It turned out pretty much as expected," says [Participant 3]. These kids, when approaching the problem, "don't apply concepts they learned in the classroom."

[Participant 4] comments that "middle-school students did as much deeper thinking as [did] high school students." She expected more sophisticated reasoning from older students. But "many older students wrote down a formula and stopped," unable to answer more.

Individual reactions include annoyance and disbelief, horror, a resigned "ho

The message subject is deliberately provocative. The tensions in the responses are brought up for discussion at the start. Opposing views are important for dialogue. The nature of the conceptual opposition should be explored, not necessarily with the goal of resolving it.

In this case, there are several different levels of expectation about the nature of assessment and questions. What does one expect of students from questions? Right answers are an obvious response, but are other levels of understanding possible or even desirable?

hum," and surprise at unsuspected patterns.

Each respondent reveals also his or her own expectation of the student response to the probes. It might be as useful to consider one or more reactions that are not yours and explore what you see as the expectations of assessments and the reasons behind the posted reactions. Do these ideas resonate with your own reactions? Why? Or why not?

The moderator concludes by characterizing responses and inviting participants to consider the expectations evident in the response of another person.

If these results were the responses to an online version of TIMSS, the international science and math test, would they be different?

To explore common ground, the moderator references standard exams like TIMSS.

USING STRATEGIES AND VOICES: WHY AND HOW?

Perhaps you see this system of voices and strategies to frame communications as rather complicated. After all, there are six strategies, six voices, with thirty-odd combinations. Can't simply responding directly to issues be more effective and efficient?

Variety is central to the rationale for using the different voices and strategies. We've found that most facilitators bring to online discussions one, two, or at most three different approaches. By having more options — including options you can use for specific effects or to address certain difficulties — you can shorten your compositions as well as the time you spend composing. Just as a counselor approaches a counseling situation with a wide variety of professional strategies like those formulated by Jung, Rogers, Skinner, Burn, or Dreikurs, you the moderator can also enter into dialogues with valuable skills in recognizing recurrent patterns, and a variety of strategies to choose from as determined by the evolution of a given dialogue. Using these strategies and voices provides three advantages: Professional distance, a framework to construct or recraft postings, and a model for clarity and effectiveness.

Your stance as "Guide on the Side" does bring added reflection. And some moderators find that it constrains the range of methods of interchange. But the personal tutor or lecturer modes do not transfer well to web-based media. The strategies we've described in this chapter offer you multiple ways to gain a professional distance from participants' exchanges, identify patterns, and compose interventions. Using strategies you normally may not employ, or that may seem awkward in face-to-face discussion, helps you reconceptualize and broaden your role as an engaged nurturer of others' thinking.

These strategies can also provide scaffolding for criticizing and revising draft interventions. The rationale and frame for intervention design emerge from context. As the moderator, you can reshape and refine the container for the intervention using appropriate strategies (as well as voices and tones).

Additionally, these strategies place helpful constraints on you as an intervention author. You must use one voice and one critical thinking strategy throughout a single intervention. The attention of readers is a precious commodity. The framework of the strategies and voices offers you guidance on what parts of a communication carry important information and which ones do not. Guided by the selection of a voice and a critical thinking strategy, your interventions will wander less, and you can make clearer the purpose for their presence in the dialogue.

There are two general methods for using the voice and critical thinking strategy framework. One might be termed the from the ground up method. To use a "ground up" construction in an intervention, you read recent entries in the dialogue and determine a rationale for your intervention. You then formulate a desired effect for the intervention. The method is similar to a traditional composition. Possible voice and critical thinking strategies guide the construction of your intervention.

Here's a brief summary of the process steps for a *from-the-ground-up* intervention:

1. Rationale	What is the rationale for the post? What purpose does it serve? Is the group getting socially focused? Are focus and direction unraveling? Are the participants "wallowing in the shallows"? Given an intervention now, what might be the result? Is the timing sensible?
2. Dialogue elements	What dialogue elements (citations, paraphrases, or quotes from participants' postings) might fit into your post? How

2. Dialogue elements (continued)	do these elements relate to rationale for the post, the assignment, and the direction of the dialogue?
3. Voice	Given your rationale and selected dialogue elements, which voice best reflects your diagnosis of what the dialogue needs?
4. Critical-Thinking Strategy	Given your rationale, the dialogue elements you've selected, and the voice you've chosen, what critical thinking strategy will best support your purpose? Do you need to help the group sharpen the focus or dig deeper? Consider an alternative voice and perhaps an alternative strategy to clarify your choices.
5. Tone	Consider what tone fits best with your rationale, dialogue elements, strategy, and voice. Is a social frame or introduction needed?
6. Outline the post	Roughly outline, perhaps mentally, the proposed posting, including elements you've drawn from the dialogue.
7. Craft the intervention	Compose the post. The purpose of the note should be clearly reflected through the critical-thinking strategy and voice you've selected. You may wish to try out an alternative voice or strategy to see if it might fit better. Remind yourself that questions are not the only tools at your disposal; you can paraphrase, seek clarification, cite tensions, introduce a metaphor or tale, or use a drawing or cartoon.
8. Reflect participants' contributions	Participants' thoughts and questions should be prominent in the body of your composition. The post should be a reflection of their ideas, not yours.
9. Craft a message title	Compose an opening and title (subject line) that catch participants' interest, honor participants' contributions, and crisply transition to the content of the post.
10. Review and revise	Review the composition process, starting with your rationale. Can the composition achieve your intended purpose? Is it too broad, too narrow, too complex, too simplistic? Does it effectively weave and focus participants' ideas or open them to a deeper level? Revise your post to answer these questions.

In an alternative, *craft-and-polish,* approach, you simply draft your posting without considering voice or strategy. Then, you go back and rewrite your message, guided by the voice and critical-thinking strategy that seem optimal given the goal of your intervention. In this case, you essentially go through the same initial steps, settling on a rationale and identifying material you'll include in the composition. Next, you choose a general frame for the intervention and decide whether your composition will sharpen participants' focus or push them to a greater depth of engagement. You then compose your intervention to suit your vision, your fancy, and the need disclosed in the dialogue. As a separate step, you can then apply a specific voice and critical-thinking strategy.

Whichever way you apply the voice and critical-thinking strategy framework, it will help you move from a central position in online discussion to a "Guide on the Side," so that you have multiple ways to craft interventions and guide discussions for clarity and effectiveness. You'll also be disciplined in sticking with just one rationale for intervening at a time. While your natural tendencies might lead you to unwittingly interrupt progress, sticking with a clear purpose for leveraging a dialogue to a more focused or deepened target will maximize your effectiveness as facilitator.

Chapter Eight

ROADBLOCKS AND GETTING BACK ON TRACK

▶

Much as in a face-to-face setting, you can encourage dialogue among the participants in an online course by collecting their ideas and focusing attention on them, or by pointing out places or means to dig deeper into them. On the other hand, you may, from time to time, unintentionally block further development of ideas.

This chapter explores a set of common interactions in written communication that can hinder or even derail the dialogue process. In some cases, you the moderator need make only minor adjustments to rectify your efforts. This fine-tuning might involve a simple shift in your voice or tone. If, for instance, you select a voice you don't often use, you can recraft one of your posts so that it highlights participants' thoughts and places your opinions in a minor role. Or perhaps, during a reread of your post before submission, you might pay careful attention to the overall impact and appearance of your entry and decide to rewrite it so that you articulate clearly and succinctly the purpose of your intervention and the critical-thinking strategy that frames it. In this "Guide on the Side" manner, you can reveal participants' thoughts to themselves in new and intriguing ways.

Other blocks to dialogue are more serious, and so they require more than your simply editing a post during a redrafting session. In these cases, the motives for your interventions unintentionally conflict with your desire to cultivate pragmatic dialogue. Online dialogue presents unique challenges. Lacking immediate feedback that you might get from students' facial expressions or body language in the classroom, you may not be aware of the effects, or the *perceived* effects, of your efforts.

Seeing themselves as nominal leaders of a discussion group, course, or workshop, facilitators commonly exhibit a tendency to jump directly into dialogues to add support to a view, thus joining into the action more as participants than as outside facilitators. The timing of your interventions and their effects is very different in online interactions. Your interventions can unwittingly interrupt the flow of text-based conversation in which postings maintain a presence that differs greatly from a passing nod or quick comment face to face. Wait time — the time it takes for ideas to percolate through readers' minds — is measured in days, not seconds, in asynchronously posted text conversation. Jumping right into the fray is generally ill advised if your goal is to support the extension of others' ideas and participants' ownership of the discussion.

But as a "Guide on the Side," you're not a mere bystander either. You must assess the timing and the forms of interventions and target them to address the specific needs of a dialogue. Communication through a text medium forces participants to clarify and commit to ideas. Identifying important ideas and trends and bringing them to the group's attention are fundamental to any process of dialogue facilitation.

Based on our work with online courses at The Concord Consortium, we've identified two general ways you can potentially impede dialogue development and move a discussion away from participant-centered inquiry toward directed responses. We characterize them as:

- "Hijacking the Dialogue"
- "Whoosh, It Went Right By"

Let us now look at each of these potentially troublesome concerns.

HIJACKING THE DIALOGUE

Though the term "hijacking" may sound a bit harsh, the process of taking over a discussion is quite tempting. Facilitators fall into this trap frequently, in both online and face-to-face settings.

Hijacking the dialogue centers around control. Many facilitators are quite comfortable remaining in the middle of a discussion, guiding discourse crisply and caringly toward a predetermined (by the facilitator) outcome. After all, it can be very gratifying to see your own ideas as benefiting the group's progress. Some group members may welcome a moderator who assumes this role. Participants gain comfort and assurance in reading the brilliant or clever lecture.

Participants' satisfaction, however, is an inadequate substitute for their personal interaction with ideas, especially if you the moderator truly seek to encourage pragmatic dialogue. Participants (more so than you) must examine glossed over comments and probe the reasoning behind their assumptions and beliefs. Though there are some cases in which a discussion, gone far astray, is in need of your immediate attention and redirection, you must carefully consider not only the potential of your intervention deepening the dialogue, but also its potential for taking the control of content and direction away from participants.

There are many ways you can exert control over a dialogue and unintentionally begin to hijack it. We've identified four basic patterns or roles that we refer to as:

- The good student
- The question mill
- Standing in the middle
- The inquiry advocate

Let's look at examples of these roles, as well as more effective strategies with respect to each.

The Good Student

One of the most difficult patterns for some moderators to recognize is the stance of moderator as *good student*. The good student is a skilled respondent who is a valued member of the class. The moderator exhibiting a good student behavior effectively sets up an unnecessary and potentially harmful competition in his or her attempt to further dialogue or the exploration of ideas.

Teacher trainers often remark that the brightest and most able students often experience considerable difficulties in their first placements as teachers. The diligence, attention seeking, and strong self-image that in the past rewarded them with teacher approval and fine grades are not traits that help others — i.e., students — to personally interact with ideas.

Professional trainers often experience a similar problem in their temptations to take control of the computer mouse, or even direct the next steps in a process. Needless to say, both of these scenarios can stand in the way of participants' learning.

Though essential to your function as a moderator or trainer, your manifest sense of personal accomplishment with electronic media, and/or your visible facility to wrestle with challenges, can intimidate beginning users. Worse, as a means of establishing a position, these strengths of yours can stake out intellectual ground and compete with participants' personal explorations. Remember: Competition is a form of self-advocacy. It certainly has a place in classrooms and in business and social forums. But you, as a facilitator of dialogues, must *facilitate*, not compete.

Here's an example of a moderator entering a dialogue as a good student, with its attending sense of competition:

Example 8.1 Rationale and Context

In one segment of INTEC, teachers studied specific software and piloted it both privately and with small groups of students. The moderator facilitated the participants' discussion and learning with comments on how learning with inquiry could be adapted to the participants' classroom environments. Postings ranged widely, from content questions to pedagogy to requests for technical help. The moderator decided to intervene to give a feeling of support and accomplishment. No specific voice or critical thinking strategy emerged in the posting.

Original Moderator Post

MESSAGE SUBJECT: What Good is This Stuff? Where Are the Problems?

Hi,

I've had a great time working through the examples teachers have come up with. Teaching algebra with technology can be a challenge, but it's such fun. I'm going to try some of these ideas out when I get the chance.

[Participant 1] mentioned how he has worked with sines and cosines in the past using Maple, MathCAD, and some

The moderator starts with a social introduction. His tone is upbeat. But he portrays himself as one of the participants doing the exercises along with the other participants, yet relying on a much more advanced skill set.

neat ideas. I've used both of these packages extensively in my teaching. I'm the local expert on Maple and Mathematica where I teach. If you want, I can share some activity files that have worked for me.

[Participant 2] and [Participant 3] remarked on how their students bumped up against the function concept and its notation. That is a tough issue for some students. It doesn't look much like any other notation they've seen before, does it?

In standard packages like Maple, MathCAD, or Mathematica, you'll need, I've discovered, to spend a lot of time on understanding the syntax of the expression. These packages don't use quite the same notation that one uses on the blackboard.

What do others do when they face notation and comprehension issues?

The moderator's expertise, though helpful in interpreting problems, can encourage a "wait 'til the answers float by" attitude among the participants.

The moderator presents his solutions, and not those of the participants, for comment. He competes for intellectual space in the dialogue.

Example 8.1 Commentary on the Original Post

The moderator enters the conversation not as a facilitator but as a peer-expert. He mentions participant entries only in passing. He devotes most of the space to chat about his — and not the participants' — accomplishments with the tools. The participants might very well be left with the sense that this person has "been there, done that; I should just sit back and listen." The voice is that of a veteran or an expert informing the rest of the participants. There is no critical thinking strategy.

The response is rewritten below, using a making-connections critical-thinking strategy with the voice of a Conceptual Facilitator. Whimsy is used to lighten up a rather heavy conceptual load. This post should also make connections with the central question of the assignment: "What value does technology add?"

Example 8.1 Recrafted Posting

MESSAGE SUBJECT: Recognizing a Horse of a Different Color

Hi,

Working with this technology does force one to revisit some old ideas! One wonders what new conclusions arise to old questions.

[Participant 1] mentions how he has "worked with sines and cosines in the past using Maple, MathCAD, and Mathematica." He likes Maple for his advanced students. He notes that the package we are studying, Measurement in Motion, "presents a very different approach to the idea of functions. ... MIM uses movies as data sources. Will the students recognize the function idea in a visual form?"

[Participant 2] and [Participant 3] remark on how their students bumped up against the function concept and its notation. [Participant 1] remarks that "the f(x), with its parentheses, doesn't look much like any other notation they've seen before." [Participant 2] notes that "they [students] memorize series of symbols with little understanding."

The idea of function keeps popping up all over the place in mathematics, and its notation does change.

$$f(x) \quad F(x) \quad F(G(x)) \quad F:=> 2x+2$$

That function "horse" keeps switching colors!

[Participant 1], [Participant 2], and [Participant 3] put their fingers on a key issue — recognizing the concept of function beyond its notation. MIM, with its visual representation through movies, offers a new way to "see" functions in the real world. How do you think you can capitalize on that potential? Or is it worth the effort to include it in your class?

The moderator acknowledges that old ideas about functions, including notation, are important. Participant quotes are prominent. The language is not that of a peer-expert. Participant concerns drive the framing of the post.

The moderator juxtaposes the problems associated with both new and traditional forms of expressing functions. Implicit is the idea that technology adds more layers to the representation issue.

The post pushes participants to look beyond particular issues like technology or notation to the more general usefulness of a conceptual approach to teaching and learning about functions.

The Question Mill

Questions demand attention. Thus, participants can easily confuse the questions in your *question mill* with those of a main assignment or agenda. Perhaps worse, your questions can override views raised by the participants.

The amount of attention any participant can devote to responding to or even considering questions at more than a superficial depth is quite limited. So if you're the type of moderator who is captivated with questions as key elements of an intervention, you'll pose a double challenge to your group's participants. For starters, your questions will likely wrest control of the dialogue away from its contributors. They'll also threaten to dilute participants' attention and focus, even if each of your questions is well-framed and within the group's field of interest. The attention participants must give to your barrage of questions will sap one of their essential resources: Their capacity to reflect. Your questions become distracting noise, and you then hijack the discussion to nowhere.

A more useful approach is to employ a voice and a critical-thinking strategy that enable you to set out an "answer mill" that includes answers gleaned from participants' entries or your own musings. Such a post can then explore the ways in which participants feel these suggestions are answers, or the assumptions and beliefs that make these suggestions answers.

Here's an example of a posting in which the moderator's questions got the upper hand:

Example 8.2 Rationale and Context

A respondent had posted a note that was conceptually rich enough to potentially unite other themes in the thread. The fine ideas in the note, however, were buried in social context. The moderator elected to craft a post to highlight the insights and drive the dialogue deeper. No recognizable tone, voice, or critical-thinking strategy was evident. Other than generating a list of questions in an already rich dialogue, the purpose of the intervention is unclear. The list of questions, no matter how interesting, confuses the discussion and ownership of its direction. The useful insight remains buried. Besides questions from the assignment and those contained in their own postings, participants now have a third set of driving questions to explore.

Example 8.2 Original Moderator Post

MESSAGE SUBJECT:
Digging Deeper for Explanations

On February 16, [Participant 1] mentioned how difficult it is for a teacher to access what a student files away deep within the brain. That got me thinking: What does INTEC offer that would help teachers access those stored nuggets? Do students feel (as teachers do) that they are on a fast-moving treadmill with no time to reflect? If we take a "less is more" attitude and provide time to reflect, to compose, to share, would these nuggets come to a conscious level, helping both the student who retrieves them and those who then receive them?

How important is learning from peers now, and how important could such learning become if the principles of INTEC were carried out on a planned, sustained basis?

[Moderator]

The moderator starts with a quote from a participant but then builds on his personal reflections, not on those of the participants. There is sufficient material in the dialogue to quote or paraphrase so that participants' ideas may be grounded in their own comments. This flurry of questions, no matter how interesting, does not come from the participants. And it clogs forward movement.

Example 8.2 Commentary on the Original Post and Its Recrafting

An intervention should not be a vehicle for expressing your personal reflections on issues. The moderator in this example needs to remove the flurry of questions as well as the elements addressing his own reflections. Several of the posts in the thread were very rich. In the recrafted moderator message, the moderator cites segments of these posts to bring a wider palette of contributions to the attention of the group. He uses a key points critical-thinking strategy with the voice of Conceptual Facilitator. The dialogue needs clarity and focus. Digging deeper on issues will come later. The moderator places two concepts in the forefront: The tension between coverage and time, and collaboration in the course to find new ways of teaching. The moderator also encourages a sharing of ideas, and he includes a humorous image to bring a lighter tone to the post. The metaphor also invites a lighter approach to notes exploring negative consequences, like slammed doors and pinched fingers and toes.

Example 8.2 Recrafted Posting

MESSAGE SUBJECT:
Opening What Doors?
To What Nuggets? [Participant 1],
[Participant 2], [Participant 3]

[Participant 1] remarked, "Too often, students fail to make connections. They memorize some info, take a test, and either promptly forget it or file it away somewhere, deep within the brain, that is difficult to access."

Later he asks, "Unfortunately, we are on such a tight schedule it's hard to fit this in. DO you find time to incorporate stuff like this in? If so, HOW????"

[Participant 2] comments in a similar vein: "It is just that there is a great deal of information to be covered in the [genetics] unit, and it moves relatively quickly."

[Participant 3] sees the student buying into the modeling software as useful, but wonders "if my testing can assess what they've really learned in the limited time I can use it."

That old tension of testing — coverage vs. time to explore — surfaces so often. We all, including students, feel that we're on a fast track to somewhere with not much time to reflect on the "nuggets," as [Participant 3] terms them.

Is there some way in which this tool, Genscope, and our collective explorations can "open the door" to this knotty problem and make the "nuggets" more available to students, bringing them to the surface for teachers to assess what was learned?

Participant quotes are prominent throughout this post. The language of the intervention draws heavily on insights captured in the participants' own words.

The moderator honors the tension between coverage and depth — a continuing issue in the dialogue — and he places it centrally in the posting.

The moderator uses humor to encourage sharing about the problem. The "fast track" metaphor captures the tensions participants have expressed. Participants had voiced their approval of the software, but they hadn't clearly articulated what exactly intrigued them and what new capacity and value the software brought to genetics teaching.

Standing in the Middle

The phrase "Guide on the Side" is appealing to many educators and trainers. Learners taking control of their questioning and interacting on their own with challenging content are the signs of real learning. But if you've worked as a teacher or trainer before, you well know that it isn't easy to move out of the center and have learners take over.

Lecterns embody the "Sage-on-the-Stage" model. The online medium admits no lecterns, of course. But even so, your language and modes of interaction as moderator can cultivate, knowingly or otherwise, an environment in which your presence is inappropriately central to the life of the dialogue. Conventions, or even connotations of language, can push or even invite you to be "center stage" when being out of the spotlight would be much more effective.

Beyond competing for center stage and crafting a flurry of questions, you can also block paths to deepening the dialogue among participants by introducing unnecessary praise, promoting your personal values, or mediating ideas by interpreting them through your own personal experiences.

Take praise, for instance. Praise, after all, conveys value. And so in the act of praising, you place your values or preferences in the center. Neither your praise nor your comments are, in and of themselves, harmful. But such efforts *must* be geared toward furthering the progress of an individual and/or the group. How can you do this? One effective strategy is to highlight the importance of participants' ideas as measured by their recurrence and value as intellectual coinage in the dialogue. Participants' contributions, emphasized in this manner, are thus praised because they're useful to the group.

Using your personal experiences can place additional roadblocks in front of the participants and their discussions. Though undoubtedly seminal in your own career or development, your thesis/dissertation topics, recollections of outstanding meetings or seminars, or recountings of various illuminating readings or environments all set up your experiences as mediating those of the participants. Your moderator-centered elements can offer important sidelights or color to a posting. But try to keep the central focus on the participants' experiences as you recount them in written dialogue and reflect upon them through your interventions.

You must constantly be aware of the potential for your communications to put you "center stage." A good question to ask yourself when you're in the process of crafting a response is, "Were this post brilliantly written, even more so than it is now, would its perspective and motivation come from a *facilitator* or from a *lecturer*?" You must seriously entertain the idea that your posts may be perceived as competitive, or that they may be motivated by your desire to demonstrate knowledge or content skill instead of facilitating the development of the participants' ideas.

Here's an example of a well-designed post whose language, in some segments, brought the moderator to a central and unnecessarily evaluative role:

Example 8.3 Rationale and Context

One participant offered some particularly insightful reflections. She engaged in exactly the kind of inquiry and personal risk taking necessary to build meaning in pragmatic dialogue. She modeled the same reflective practice as the teacher in the video clip that was part of the assignment. The important segment of her post, however, was buried in content and social surroundings. The moderator elected to highlight this reflection for the group to experience. The critical thinking strategy used is unclear. The *key-points* approach implies multiple points and contributions. This lengthy post is closest to a *sorting-for-relevance* approach. The tone is neutral. The post is reduced to a couple of quotes. Other themes from the post are left for another time. The citations take the spirit of the assignment and push it to its limits. There is no need to broaden the question base or use any of the more complex critical thinking strategies to leverage a deeper dialogue. Looking more carefully at the wealth in these ideas is all that's necessary.

Example 8.3 Original Moderator Post

MESSAGE SUBJECT: [Participant 1], [Participant 2], and Giving Credit

I just loved the question with which [Participant 1] ended her post. After going on at some length about the frustration of time and objectives and quantity being valued over quality in school (perhaps especially among college prep students), she suddenly stepped back to wonder: "How did I

The moderator unnecessarily inserts herself and her values into the commentary. Pleasing the moderator is irrelevant. Instead of commenting, it's better to hold the bold and elegant reflection up for clearer view.

really know that they could not figure out a word problem in time to cover all of the examples I had planned?" That is, she began to search herself after letting out that steam. She used the video as a reflection tool — for her, [Participant 2] models giving "kids a lot of credit for figuring out things for themselves."

What have others noticed [Participant 2] modeling? What has been learned about ourselves and our teaching?

Example 8.3 Commentary on the Original Post

Participants should not see their efforts as means to please you. Thus, in the rewritten effort below, the focus of the posting highlights the moment of wonder experienced by the teacher. The same critical-thinking strategy, sorting for relevance, is evident. The Reflective Guide voice that's used always carries a Rogerian quality — a thought commenting on itself through another. [Participant 1's] insight is bold. The voice of a Reflective Guide can highlight these important reflections and the rationale for communicating them. The intention of the Reflective Guide is to reveal participants' thinking and, through the intervention, bridge that thinking to other participants. The moderator remembers, in the final paragraph, the sense of community and comfort that permitted the teacher to contribute these reflections.

Example 8.3 Recrafted Post

MESSAGE SUBJECT: [Participant 1], [Participant 2], and Giving Credit

After commenting on the frustration of time, objectives, and quantity being valued over quality in school (perhaps especially among college prep students), [Participant 1] suddenly stepped back to wonder. She ended her post with this provocative question: "How did I really know that they could not figure out a word problem in time to cover all of the examples I had planned?"

The moderator briefly reviews the contents of the posts instead of summarizing them. The language here is descriptive and neutral. The moderator honors the question by putting it last, then redescribes, in a Rogerian manner, [Participant 1's] experience and insights. The quote remains prominent.

This question seems to indicate that the process of watching and reflecting on the video opened [Participant 1] to surfacing her own perhaps limiting assumptions about herself and her students. She states: "We tend to look at something in one way and we don't take the time or the brain power to consider all options. I also tend to not give my kids a lot of credit for figuring out things for themselves."

Details of the post are the centerpiece of commentary.

[Participant 1's] phrase "not giving credit for figuring things out" echoes a form of intellectual trust in the students and oneself as a teacher. Cultivating this quality seems necessary, but a real challenge. [Participant 1], in our dialogue, and [Participant 2], the teacher in the video, took risks in talking openly about their practices.

The post ends with an affirmation of the need for trust in dialogue about inquiry, as well as an invitation to join in with more insights. The moderator also revisits questions from the assignment.

What other assumptions about teaching and learning can be gleaned from watching [Participant 2] with his students and carefully reflecting on your own practice?

What relevant chords did [Participant 2's] and [Participant 1's] experiences strike?

The Inquiry Advocate

Taking over content isn't the only way you the moderator can dominate a conversation; you can also take over the discussion's process.

In the "negotiating space" phase of a dialogue, there's always an exploration of the motives and process of the expected conversation. As Senge (1990) notes, there is a tension between advocacy of any position and the process of inquiry. Through inquiry, participants in a dialogue seek to examine assumptions, beliefs, or possibilities, without defending or placing value on them. Outward agreement can mask very different perceptions or rationales for participants' statements or positions.

177

In transitioning from social or argumentative forms of dialogue to pragmatic dialogue, participants must move beyond advocating their personal views or solutions so that they can engage in open inquiry. Senge describes this activity as probing what options are available and what beliefs or assumptions support existing opinions or positions. As facilitator, then, you can find yourself in the uncomfortable position of being perceived as advocating the use of inquiry as a better way to communicate. Such an *inquiry advocate* can defeat the purpose of the dialogue.

Advocating any topic or process evokes in many people some level of overt opposition; in many other people it produces persistent passive resistance. People don't like to be told, "Do this!" or, "This is better than what you're doing." If one advocates for freedom of the press, for instance, a common response is "the press can't print everything." Indeed, the press can't. Dialogue might then ensue to clarify the meaning of "freedom of the press" and individual rights and responsibilities. Subsequent dialogue might ask participants, in the spirit of inquiry, to suspend judgments or commitments to personal beliefs or positions and examine alternate perspectives.

If you the moderator are perceived as taking a position of advocating inquiry, some participants might see the process of inquiry as a party line or as a channel to learning that they can narrow or block. In other words, participants can interpret your interventions as billboards in the scenery that proclaim, "Do it my way!"

Thus, a sense of neutrality, a "wait and see" skepticism, or downright ambivalence about commitment to the truth or the validity of certain statements fits well with an inquiry model, more than a "this-is-the-way-to-go" approach does. Participants should feel free to challenge the value of any approach, including one based on inquiry. Let participants affirm the validity and usefulness of an inquiry-based approach on their own terms. You have the luxury of standing outside conversations and viewing, even highlighting, tensions as sources of further reflection among the participants. Reflecting on the natural resistance people feel when sensing manipulation can bring some added depth to any conversation.

However, jumping in is not necessarily the best use of uncertainty when it does emerge. The question for you is, When is a comment necessary? Was this too soon, or right on time?

With these questions in mind, consider the following intervention:

Example 8.4 Rationale and Context

The discussion area has been quite active. There have been many personal interpretations of inquiry. The moderator decides to focus the discussion by selecting the most positive elements (in her opinion) and bringing them up for discussion. The critical-thinking strategy is *key points*. The voice is unclear; it approximates a Conceptual Facilitator but doesn't directly deal with any content. Reasons for the various selections are also unclear, and the moderator fails to crisply identify ideas for reflection.

Example 8.4 Original Moderator Post

MESSAGE SUBJECT:
Inquiry? We're Doing Great!

[Participant 1] and [Participant 2] have really grappled with what inquiry means to them. "It's asking questions of oneself and others, questioning answers as well as the direction to go in." We're on a road to producing a unified view of inquiry learning and teaching.

[Participant 3] has moved on to ways to transform all of her exercises into inquiry format.

[Participant 4] has contributed some fine strategies to redesign her lessons. Congratulations. We're on the road to putting inquiry in every part of the curriculum!

[Participant 5] struggles to find out what the meaning of inquiry is for Ohio teachers. He looks at their state standards and its definition and finds ways to push his lessons in that direction.

Where is it that you are getting common ground for your meaning for inquiry?

The moderator, much like a cheerleader, selects elements of postings that all point in the same direction. Praise appears in all elements of the post, but it isn't substantive. It's not difficult to imagine a participant thinking that the moderator has a plan for where things ought to go and is praising and pushing everybody in that direction.

Example 8.4 Commentary on the Original Post

The post doesn't reveal the range of approaches and reactions to inquiry. The moderator has glossed over tensions in the postings. The strategy the moderator has chosen for the rewrite is *making connections.* The moderator examines alternative interpretations and assumptions. There are plenty of data to comment upon; the group needs to go beyond description to a deeper analysis of assumptions and beliefs. The voice here is that of a Conceptual Facilitator. The tone is analytical and neutral. Removing praise and implicit statements of advocacy places control of the conversation back in the participants' hands. The recrafted response includes comments by other participants, and it encourages participants to be comfortable with questioning and exploring assumptions.

Example 8.4 Recrafted Post

MESSAGE SUBJECT:
"Sold on Inquiry?"

Many participants took the poll.

[Participant 1] and [Participant 2] have really grappled with what inquiry means to them: "It's asking questions of oneself and others, questioning answers as well as the direction to go in." Previously they noted, in the online poll of participants, that the desired use of inquiry as "51% or more is quite high, even too high."

[Participant 3] likes the idea of "students owning the main ideas." But she wonders if this much inquiry is even good for the students. "Shouldn't a variety of styles be used?" she asks.

[Participant 4] gives her own ways to bring inquiry into lessons but highlights a contradiction and some confusion: "The majority of teachers see the value and the importance of inquiry learning. However, not everyone is using it." She wonders if we're all using the same definition: "Is inquiry just hands-on? Or is it more than that?"

The recrafted post removes the elements of praise and advocacy and holds up for view tensions in the same entries cited.

Instead of a focusing strategy, the moderator has selected a digging-deeper strategy. The composition invites reflection on reasons for the tensions or ambivalence toward the process of inquiry. Each citation admits multiple interpretations.

[Participant 5] wonders about the motivation of the poll takers: "I also found the fact that most respondents selected over 50% of class time on inquiry to be high. Are respondents attempting to tell the poll takers [INTEC] what they think they want to hear, or are they, I mean you, really sold on the idea of inquiry?!"	*The post recognizes that minds are not made up.*
[Participant 6] likes the "active questioning" but also questions the validity of this poll from another direction: "The sample is biased. Isn't this a self-selected group taking a course on inquiry?"	
[Participant 7] cites the Ohio standards and states, "I feel that I must bring many or all of these methods into my class." But he is very unsure of time commitments and "what will be the real outcome."	
There is plenty of engagement in inquiry as well as ambivalence here. Teachers are exploring what motivations lie behind their own questions. It might be helpful to examine our assumptions about teacher and student questions. Where is it that we see the added value for them? for the teacher? What assumptions or beliefs about current practice don't seem to mesh with our 51%+ support of the value of inquiry?	*The moderator's ending is not a summation inviting closure, but rather a restatement of major issues in a sequence. Instead of pushing a commonly presumed agenda, the moderator solicits participants' help in exploring the incoherence in thinking patterns.*

WHOOSH, IT WENT RIGHT BY

Hijacking represents just one pole of facilitator interaction. It's motivated by an overly active, though perhaps well-meaning, concern for direction and process. Another mode of facilitator interaction, equally effective in blocking the development of dialogue, might be characterized as a form of unconsciousness or sleepwalking, with ensuing inattention to detail, background, or context. We call this mode *whoosh, it went right by.*

If you're a moderator in "whoosh" mode, you stay on the sidelines as all kinds of interesting and potentially productive comments zip right past, like the blur of unattended scenery on a long trip. As moderator, one of your fundamental duties is highlighting patterns in dialogue. Just as flowers that seem quite bland on first inspection reveal stunning new structure and intricacy when illuminated by an ultraviolet source, your thoughtfulness, precision, and attention to detail call to a group's attention important, unseen, and unsuspected patterns.

A singular strength of online dialogue is its commitment to a text medium, which naturally focuses ideas. The medium's written transcript allows participants to review previous comments and jump in anywhere, anytime to continue a line of thought. By standing aside and not actively modeling pattern seeking, you the moderator might unknowingly assist in transforming a reflective dialogue space to a mere social arena. Your entries into a dialogue, at minimum, support a general level of wakefulness, thoughtfulness, and attention to the importance of what participants are communicating between and among each other.

The volume of material in a large dialogue space can certainly be daunting, perhaps readable only by the most dedicated facilitator. You, for example, may not be able to read all communications as thoroughly as you might wish. (You may have to simply skim some messages or leave them unopened.) Yet attention to detail in the conceptual landscape being created by the respondents is an essential function of online facilitation. If you want to move a group out of the "shallows" and into deeper dialogue, you'll need to develop skills in rapid inspection and abstraction, so that you can spot the gems of expression or metaphor and identify areas of creative tension that can drive the dialogue forward.

Your entries must convey a sense that participants are reading, listening, and reflecting on their ideas thoughtfully and carefully. Participants should sense that contributions are building meaning, and that the conceptual landscape they're exploring is emerging in finer and finer detail.

We've identified four general styles of facilitator interaction that encourage "whoosh" and its inattention to detail:

- "If I Do Nothing, They Will Inquire"
- "Summaries vs. Landscapes"
- "Letters from a Fellow Traveler"
- "The Five-Cornered Intersection"

Let us now examine each of these styles in more depth.

If I Do Nothing, They Will Inquire

When faced with the challenge of supporting inquiry in a dialogue, some moderators retire from view, believing or wishing that the invitation to talk openly will inspire the spirit of inquiry to take over. Often, though, it doesn't. Even if sufficient community building has taken place so that the group feels a sense of trust and support, engaging in pragmatic dialogue about any topic requires risk. It challenges participants to examine why they hold certain views and what beliefs and assumptions they're making to support their statements. Thus, for many reasons, participants may hesitate to commit to a public examination of the reasons behind their views, particularly in the initial phases of a dialogue. Your interventions as moderator at this point are often sorely needed.

Comments — in the form of praise — without depth or reason and made by either you or a participant can also cause disengagement from the dialogue: "I really liked the article." "I'll take these ideas and use them for sure." "Others will find the ideas beneficial." These expressions are the equivalent of head nods, smiles, or eye contact in face-to-face meetings, and they give no indication of whether participants are engaging with the ideas being presented. Thus, you may, and perhaps should, ask, and answer, using the voice of a Personal Muse: "Why?" "What is the source of its appeal?" "What, in particular, is there of value that you seek to use with your students?" The Personal Muse models the expectations for the kind of exchange and commitment to examination of reasons that are at the heart of pragmatic dialogue.

Additionally, don't be afraid to speak up and enter into a discussion that is shallow so that you can indicate potential areas of interest. Encourage participants to go beyond the face value of various statements so that they can explore the reasons people might make, and believe, such statements.

Using a form we call a "hang-your-hat post," you the moderator — facing the challenge of initiating dialogue in the early phases of a discussion — can openly muse about various meanings in an assignment, or explore tensions or key issues. The goal of such a post is to model the acts of online reflection and risk taking that are essential to any learning community.

Discussions also can degenerate into exchanges of technical tips or descriptions of environments. Elements of social dialogue are always necessary, most certainly; but they don't directly contribute to the direction defined by assignments or other substantive posts. So as moderator, you must be ready to post entries that gently but firmly move drifting or becalmed dialogues toward lines that have more potential for movement.

Here's a sample moderator intervention that adds little to the dialogue:

Example 8.5 Rationale and Context

Participants in this online course seemed reluctant to enter the dialogue, and were perhaps in need of some guidance with the interface. They didn't yet understand the moderator's expectations for contributions to the space, nor did they grasp the elements of pragmatic dialogue. The moderator post that follows was intended as a "hang-your-hat" entry, a lead-in for respondents on where and what to post for the assignment. No strategy or voice is evident. (Note: *Private Universe* refers to a film about science education by PBS/Annenberg. Viewing the film was part of the assignment.)

Example 8.5
Original Moderator Posting

MESSAGE SUBJECT:
Assignment 2A — *Private Universe*

The *Private Universe* video we saw and the Mazur article were quite interesting, I thought.

Post your comments here for Assignment 2A about the Private Universe video and the Mazur article.

The entry fundamentally says nothing. The praise is vacant. The instructions add little to support reflection or dialogue among the participants.

Example 8.5 Commentary on the Original Posting

The placeholder posting ("post your comments here") should have interacted more with the material and the participants. The main assignment, viewing the PBS video and reading an article, was conceptually rich. Ideas needed to be explored a bit and juxtaposed.

The strategy chosen for the rewrite that follows is key points. These points are simple rephrasings of the assignment itself, with a minimum of personal interaction with ideas. The voice is that of a Personal Muse. The moderator seeks to model the kind of internal reflection and gnawing on uncertainty and imprecision that can be

---

very productive for pragmatic dialogue. The tone selected is unusual in that it expresses anger, irritation, and uncertainty. The tone invites participants to share their uneasiness or frustration, and also to express more positive experiences and insights from the interaction with the materials. The posting pushes the group beyond shallow interaction with liking readings or a video to substantive dialogue about learning and conceptual change.

Example 8.5 Recrafted Posting

**MESSAGE SUBJECT: Initial
Thoughts — Mazur, PU, and Probes**

My initial thoughts about the Mazur article and viewing the *Private Universe* video were anger. I was angry with Mazur because he made me uncomfortable. I started thinking about my own teaching practices: Was I really teaching, and were my students really learning? I always thought of myself as a good teacher, but when Mazur wrote ...

The opening sentence draws the reader in. What engendered the anger? The moderator examines rationale for positions and openly expresses uncertainty about his own teaching.

"The old feeling of satisfaction turned more and more into a feeling of sadness and frustration. How could these undoubtedly bright students, capable of solving complicated problems, fail on these ostensibly 'simple' questions?"

The citations from the reading are short and well chosen. The moderator uses a convention of italics for the article quotes.

... I had the feeling that maybe all my years of teaching were a waste. The *Private Universe* video reinforced my anger. I laughed, of course, at the students' statements about where trees get their mass, but underneath I was really crying. I tried to think about why I was so angry and who I was angry at. I reread the Mazur article and thought about his solution to "expose the problem in one's own class. The key, I believe, is to ask simple questions that focus on single concepts."

Is Mazur correct? Is the "simple question" idea just too simple? "Click your heels three times, Dorothy, and you're back in Kansas." Will this help solve the problem of misinformation?

Students come into a classroom with all kinds of information about the world around them. How do we break the barriers to what they think is true? The online probes that are a part of this class also made me feel uncomfortable. Maybe because I thought I would get the answer wrong. Watching the *Private Universe* video and reviewing my students' responses to those "simple" questions made me think about the knowledge I bring with me into situations. Sometimes, no matter what evidence someone has to the contrary, you still believe you are correct.

Signed,

Your moderator (mumbling out loud?)

The moderator juxtaposes the interviews of the Private Universe *film, in which Harvard graduates voice very unscientific opinions about the origin of mass in plants. "It comes from the soil," many explain to researchers at Harvard's graduation ceremonies.*

The moderator ends by exploring the tension between "simple" questions and a person's reactions to evidence contradicting his or her beliefs about the truth.

Summaries vs. Landscapes

Summarizing is often hard to resist as a moderator. Summarizing can clarify and give participants a sense of direction. You should realize, however, that summaries also place you the moderator at the center of a dialogue — and that summaries have the potential to close doors and block paths to alternative ways of thinking. Summaries abstract ideas and place them in a hierarchy of meaning that you determine. Positions can appear to harden when you try to capture them in your summaries. And often, important nuances can disappear as you highlight contentions or assumptions instead of the reasons people have for holding them.

If you want to help participants build meaning from their discussions, a more useful intervention alternative on your part is to summarize by portraying a "landscape," which may include multiple perspectives on the issues discussed. Ambivalence or the suspension of judgment is critical for pragmatic dialogue.

Let's look at an example:

Example 8.6 Rationale and Context

In this posting, the moderator uses a daisy metaphor to craft the perfect segue to an open challenge to inquiry. The posting comes at the end of one segment of the INTEC course, a point at which participants move to crafting their own definitions of teaching with inquiry. The moderator cites and juxtaposes participants' comments with considerable skill. But the summary in the post is the weakest part. It unbalances the elegant daisy metaphor and potentially constrains reflection and sustained tension. The voice used is that of a Conceptual Facilitator. The critical-thinking strategy is *key points*. The tone is delightfully whimsical, offsetting the length and heavy content of the reflections.

Example 8.6 Original Moderator Post

MESSAGE SUBJECT:
Digging Deeper on Explanations

Hello Cohort P,

Reading through all of your wonderful posts has been like eating my Post Grapenuts cereal in the mornings. ... They have been real eye openers for me, and a great way to start my day as well as the next phase of INTEC.

There are lots of ideas and questions about the nature of inquiry. I seem to detect what I call a "daisy effect." Remember the childhood ritual of plucking petals out of a daisy and reciting, "loves me, loves me not"? I notice a similar pattern in your responses: Our current sweetheart is "inquiry" — and we recite, "love it, love it NOT"!

(This was the closest image I could find to a daisy!) We LOVE inquiry for a lot of reasons. Many of you noted that inquiry takes us beyond rote memorization.

The posting begins and continues with a healthy touch of whimsy. The task is laying out the various responses to the online poll on the value and use of inquiry in teaching. The moderator weaves her commentary and all respondents' notes into a metaphor about plucking daisies.

The moderator crisply captures contributions and groups them into "love it" and "love it NOT" categories.

The "love it NOT" group clearly sets out, in their own words, teachers' problems with inquiry teaching. The moderator notes student and teacher failures in their first contacts with inquiry.

[**Participant 1's**] "students really think when they construct their own knowledge." She thinks it "leads to more long-lasting results." [**Participant 2**] says his "students are motivated." [**Participant 3**] and [**Participant 4**] think it brings excitement, "connects to the real world," and "leads to a higher level of understanding."

Next daisy/inquiry petal please ... On the other hand — our sweetheart inquiry — **we love it NOT.** ... Students do not always take to this approach. [**Participant 1's**] students "whine at first because it is hard." [**Participant 5's**] students "don't like it because they have to think for themselves." With [**Participant 6's**] first attempts at inquiry, when she had kids design their own problems, "things didn't go well."

More NOT petals ... Having students work in groups can be difficult. [**Participant 7's**] group work has "met with mixed success." [**Participant 6**] and [**Participant 3**] wonder about group size and "equal roles for all students." [**Participant 8**] grapples with "how to prevent motivated students from taking over a group."

Many of you cited the T word — TIME. Teachers need time — to practice and to experiment with working with inquiry approaches. [**Participant 4**] uses the word "demanding" when referring to the time involved in his experiences. [**Participant 5**] worries about problems finding "the time to come up with ideas on my own." [**Participant 2's**] time for inquiry often has to be scheduled on Saturdays. [**Participant 7's**] extra time has recently been consumed by her "being in charge of homecoming festivities at her

The moderator bolds participants' names in the text to highlight individual contributions. The data from which the comments were taken were quite dispersed throughout the thread. To lay out the various ideas, the moderator collects responses for view.

Most teachers mentioned time as a central problem. Thus, the moderator devotes a large segment of her post to that issue.

school." Who said teachers get weekends off?

More "love it NOT" plucks ... [Participant 2], [Participant 8], [Participant 5], and [Participant 6] mentioned the drawback of the difficulty of doing inquiry projects in the dreaded 40-minute time block, and having to stop a good learning situation just when students seem to be gaining interest. [Participant 7] notes that she has to work with inexpensive, outdated equipment and limited access to the computer lab for Internet connections.

The moderator cites equal "love it NOT" petals as well as the main reasons for not using inquiry.

More "love it NOT" petals ... The '90s' smoking gun — ASSESSMENT! [Participant 6] wonders out loud about how to go from discovery lab to everyday, normal, end-of-chapter tests. [Participant 9] has had to defend her inquiry approach to parents and school board members who wonder where all the textbooks went. [Participant 5] and [Participant 1] also note that parents don't get it if their kids don't bring home a science or math textbook. [Participant 10] offers this advice: "Pass out the darn books, but you don't have to use them."

The moderator addresses the central issue of assessment at a personal level. She paraphrases responses for concise presentation. And she highlights the reasons for positions vs. the positions themselves.

In summary, I sense that you feel that using inquiry is demanding and hard to do, but that it is worth the work since the learning and teaching are better. I think my plucking ended on a "love it" petal. What do you think? Do you agree or disagree?

The summary is out of place considering the fine landscape the moderator set out previously. A conclusion isn't necessary; investigation and suspension of judgment are what the group really needs.

[Moderator]

Example 8.6 Commentary on the Original Post

The first part of this intervention is very well written. The moderator effectively cites and cleverly organizes participants' contributions, and she uses the *key points* strategy well. In addition, the daisy plucking metaphor has a long life in the dialogue. It becomes a shorthand for the process of suspending judgment to examine real rationales behind decision making. Encouraging the use of metaphors or language crafted to evoke specific meanings is an excellent way to build a sense of ownership of ideas. This approach works best when participants coin the phrases or generate the images; but moderator-generated phrases and images, if they're accepted and they fulfill the group's needs, can also be effective.

The moderator simply needs to rework the last paragraph of her post so that she avoids premature summarizing and doesn't compel participants to make judgments before the facts are in.

Example 8.6 Recrafted Posting (Rewritten Last Paragraph)

So what's our bottom line?
Love it -> Tally = 5
Love it not -> Tally = 5
Hmmmmmm. Score tied!

What our group seems to have individually and collectively expressed is a healthy sense of ambivalence toward inquiry.

But … ambivalence is good!

If we were all in "gung ho" mode after reading a few articles and postings and trying out some activities, I'd be a bit suspicious! Some ambivalence, skepticism, and suspension of judgment are essential to a scientific approach, and they are always involved when we're facing a potential change in our thoughts and/or behaviors. This is an excellent start. This course gives us the opportunity to put aside our judgments and preconceptions about the use and value of inquiry and to find out exactly what inquiry teaching and learning will mean for us and our classrooms.

[Moderator]

The rewritten paragraph emphasizes the variety of responses and encourages exploration of the reasons why participants hold various positions about inquiry teaching. The moderator compliments participants on their unwillingness to rush to judgment. The paragraph builds a segue to the next segment of the course — a more personal investigation of inquiry teaching.

Letter from a Fellow Traveler

Letter writing fits naturally with many forms of electronic communication. But are the form and intent of a letter a good fit with the dialogue in an online course or working group?

Pragmatic online dialogue follows a model that is closer to the give-and-take of a lively face-to-face discussion than the exchange of letters between correspondents. A letter presumes that the author has some stance and a goal of social and sometimes intellectual engagement. A letter informs the reader of the author's ideas. Your communications as a group moderator, on the other hand, must have a different purpose. Your task is to facilitate individual and collective reflection on participants' ideas — and not inject your own thoughts into the various matters of discussion.

Some may say that there are exceptions to this sweeping generalization about the nature of letters and their inapplicability to online discourse. For example, you may need to write a letter to your group detailing some issue about administration or some clarification of processes. But email may be a more appropriate vehicle for this type of communication. It's true that some letters do encourage reflection: Dr. Martin Luther King, Jr.'s "Letters from a Birmingham Jail" are salient examples. But these magnificent works, and others of similar form and intent, are really philosophical essays, not letters or forms of traditional correspondence. Their purpose is to educate a general audience and to help others engage in moral or political critiques. The *focusing-* and *digging-deeper* strategies (see Chapter 7) that lend themselves properly to online facilitating describe a much more limited role of the facilitator as a thoughtful counselor.

Letters from participants, on the other hand, are a different matter. The narrative prose that is natural to a letter may be a comfortable vehicle for some participants to use. If your moderation efforts encourage participants to engage in reflective letter writing, you've achieved your goal of deepening the dialogue.

Following is an example of a moderator communication that functions more like a letter than a facilitative entry:

191

Example 8.7 Rationale and Context

After introductions and activities exploring a personal experience of inquiry, INTEC teachers receive new inquiry-based content materials that form the basis of the rest of the course. Assignments include familiarization with the new materials and readings. The moderator here has elected to post an intervention as a bridge from previous ideas about assessment to extensions enabled by new, more "hands-on" content material. The post attempts to highlight some key ideas and set out tensions in the reading with comments in the discussion threads. The critical-thinking strategy is *key points*, though the post is overly long and the points are rather scattered. The voice is unclear. The posting reads in places more like a letter. It wanders from a personal exposition to a neutral review.

**Example 8.7
Original Moderator Posting**

MESSAGE SUBJECT: Activity Two

It's hard to believe that a month has passed and we are now well into February. The snow has melted and we are anticipating some cold weather to return before the winter passes. How are things in your area?

You have probably had some great experiences with your students this past month as you began the section of INTEC where you learned new content tools. It always seems that theory takes on a new look once it is embedded into the real curriculum we present to kids. What we think will happen may, but there are always those unexpected surprises or "Ohhhhh, now I get it!" moments. I'm looking forward to reading your posts on the assessment component of this experience. Most administrators are concerned that we "prove" students learned from the classroom experiences we facilitate. <grin> When too much time is spent with pencil-and-paper tests, we lose valuable time for exploration and inquiry. But we are educators, and therefore we must answer to someone for the

After some social chitchat about the weather, the moderator acknowledges accomplishments to date. She brings in language from previous discussions (e.g., "unexpected surprises," concerns of administrators) to "prove" citation.

The moderator entertains the perennial tensions of content coverage and testing. Importantly, she resists the temptation to summarize.

the learning that takes place in the school. :-)

Linda Dager Wilson says that authentic assessment "encompasses a broad range of criteria, but performance remains an essential aspect." Did you find that your students were able to perform using their newly learned knowledge, or were they still answer-oriented? How did you measure their success (or learning)?

The moderator visits an assignment on authentic assessment, but she asks a different question than the ones in the assignment.

There are still large numbers of educators who have taught students with traditional, textbook-driven methods. Many of these educators have seen their students score well on ACT/SAT tests, graduate from prominent universities, and continue their lives as very productive citizens. Why should these folks change their teaching techniques and/or assessment practices? What arguments would you give to convince that "traditional" teacher to try something you have experienced in INTEC? Did you find a particular assessment technique that seemed efficient, captured the interest of the student, and/or demonstrated students' ability to perform based on their learning concepts rather than facts?

The moderator cites the tension between traditional teaching and newer methods and links that tension to standardized testing practices. She also asks more questions (which are also not from the assignment). The questions are good, but they lose their meaning as they pile up on each other.

Enjoy the module and materials you're working with. We'll be continuing our assessment for a couple of months. Good luck, and have a great time with your students.

[Moderator]

Example 8.7 Commentary on the Original Posting

The original posting brings in personal commentary and too many questions, many of them rhetorical, that confuse the assignment. The moderator honors the legacy of participants' ideas from previous threads, but not directly. In a style much like that of a response letter, the moderator responds to the comments instead of highlighting and juxtaposing them to make issues and tensions stand out.

The rewritten posting that follows uses the same critical-thinking strategy, *key points*. The moderator weaves article terms into the language used by the participants in previous discussions. The voice here is that of a Conceptual Facilitator. The moderator highlights specific quotations or paraphrases for reflection and commentary. A neutral, second- and third-person approach is predominant, and the letter-like style is gone.

Example 8.7 Recrafted Posting

MESSAGE SUBJECT:
Assessment, New Tools,
and What DO We Know They Know?

Hello Cohort S,

It's hard to believe that a month has passed. Snow has melted but winter may return, our weatherman says. Hope you'll fare better.

You've probably had some great experiences in the last month with your own piloting of materials or work with a few willing students, as you began the section of INTEC where you learn to teach with new tools. [Participant 1], [Participant 2], [Participant 3], and [Participant 4] have given hints of both success and failure in their first attempts. It always seems that the theory of working with inquiry takes on a new look once it's embedded into the real curriculum we must present to kids.

Linda Dager Wilson's article brings up what [Participant 5] called the 'A' word: Assessment. What a pesky thorn that one is! [Participant 6] asks, "How DO we

After the salutation, the moderator mentions, but doesn't summarize, the experiences of the previous assignments. She recalls the product of the course: The seeking of practical answers to real problems. The letter-like quality of the original post has given way to a key points form.

The moderator re-poses questions directly from the assignment or article.

know what they really learned?" [Participant 7] wonders, "Authentic assessment — what could that really mean?" Did the tool you worked with give new options?

We've all taught with traditional methods at one time or another. [Participant 8] notes that our students, taught by "older methods," enter "into college with good scores on ACT/SATs." She remarks that, in a way, these approaches have proven their value. The assignment asks, "What added value can these other assessment efforts bring us?" Linda Wilson and Ms. League in the article give some insights and challenges.

The moderator revisits ideas about the ACT/SAT and "proven" traditional techniques of assessment. She also restates the issue of valuing assessment.

If students do poorly on authentic assessment formats, does this mean they really can't apply the knowledge they know in multiple-choice formats — or do they just not value it?

The final question repeats a key tension between authentic and traditional assessment, in a form paraphrased from participants' comments.

[Moderator]

The Five-Cornered Intersection

Quality facilitation demands attention to detail. But the details you cull need to make collective sense and contribute to a wider vision for the dialogue. In selecting segments of posts for quotes, you need to choose wisely. And when you ultimately compose your message, you must knit the ideas and insights from each contributor into a coherent platform for further thinking.

If you select and comment upon disconnected pieces without pulling ideas together, your communication will leave the impression of imprecision and disconnected design — not unlike like a *five-cornered intersection*. Readers will sense some familiarity and continuity, but they'll also stop to wonder, "What is the purpose of this collection?" Not because they're interested but because they're confused, they'll ask, "Where does any of this lead?"

In an asynchronous environment, participants often see their own responses as letters or notes that contribute to a lengthening list of commentary. In trying to build deeper discussion, you should keep an eye out for commonalties in groups of responses; you can even go so far as to include interesting comments from previous threads that were never picked up. You can then use these materials to weave a post that highlights commonalties and tensions.

Here's a post that attempts to build on interesting comments but fails to connect them coherently:

Example 8.8 Rationale and Context

The dialogue had been going slowly in this group. Participants are studying *VideoPoint*, a software program. It permits analysis of *Quicktime*™ movies for math and science classrooms. A difficulty emerged early in the discussion: Participants seemed to jump in and offer comments, often rather technically focused, without much reference to others' efforts. So the moderator decided to craft a posting that acknowledged contributions and worked toward building more content interactions. The moderator selected three contributions for comment. Which voice she chose isn't clear. The format of quotes from a participant plus an added question is not a *key points* strategy. This post fragments, rather than unifies, the directions for discussion.

Example 8.8 Original Moderator Post

MESSAGE SUBJECT:
Further Thoughts

Here are a few thoughts from Activity 2 that your comments have generated. There are a number of things to think about. A big part of inquiry is to dig deeper into the issues, so here are a few points we might want to dig into.

The invitation to "dig into" inquiry, though important and implicit in the discussion, is framed as coming from the moderator.

[Participant 1] commented, after looking at the karate clip (on the *VideoPoint* CD): "Of course, we (our class) would talk about how accurate their original guesses were at the conclusion, and what misconceptions they had."

Quotes from [Participant 1] and [Participant 2] address different issues. [Participant 1] describes conjectures, verification, and identifying misconceptions. [Participant 2] describes technical issues regarding uncertainty in visual data collection.

Thought 1: What misconceptions do we as educators think our students might have? What are misconceptions?

In [Participant 2's] response to [Participant 1's] post, he mentioned: "It (the karate clip) has a lot of potential, but it was so hard to see the hand at some times that I was guessing about where to mark it for analysis."

The two thoughts don't link [Participant 1's] and [Participant 2's] comments, nor do they relate to the assignment.

Thought 2: How do we help students identify errors that they have made when marking videos? What do we get them to look for?

[Participant 2] also raised a point about modeling using SIN and COS to determine angular speed constants. He said: "I tend to do it by trial and error. On the plus side, doing this trial and error can help students get a feeling for how this variable relates to the period of the function."

Modeling SIN and COS and errors brings in another issue.

Thought 3: How can we deepen inquiry through trial and error?

[Participant 3's] post raises an interesting point about how the use of a different technology might affect the teaching of the lesson. He shared the point that I would like to share, namely a discovery that may help some when it comes time to show the *VideoPoint* movies: "When utilizing the computer as an electronic chalkboard, I connect my computer to a 27-inch TV monitor."

Thought 4: How might the use of a technology (working at a monitor vs. presenting on a large TV) help or hinder inquiry?

The final comment addresses a fourth topic: the use of technology.

Any thoughts so far?

[Moderator]

The posting leaves considerable confusion as to where to go next. Where would a participant begin to respond?

Example 8.8 Commentary on the Original Posting

The original posting is long and confusing. The paraphrases or extensions of participants' thoughts, numbered "Thought One" through "Thought Four," don't deepen the discussion but instead potentially divide it. The moderator makes no connections to the assignment.

Below, the post is recrafted using a *sorting-for-relevance* strategy with the voice of a Conceptual Facilitator. The same quotations appear, but they're reflected through the central question of the assignment.

Example 8.8 Recrafted Posting

MESSAGE SUBJECT:
Where's the Value (Beef)?

Comments regarding the main theme of these threads — "Where is the value added by this technology?" — have been wide-ranging.

The moderator acknowledges the wide-ranging nature of the responses. Participants' quotes carry the main ideas. There are no paraphrased or extended questions.

[Participant 1] commented: "Of course, we (our class) would talk about how accurate their original guesses were at the conclusion and what misconceptions they had."

[Participant 2] responded to [Participant 1]: "It (the karate clip) has a lot of potential, but it was so hard to see the hand at some times that I was guessing about where to mark it for analysis."

The moderator crisply cites four areas of interest: conjectures and misconceptions, uncertainty about data, "old" methods giving a feeling that new methods cannot, and new forms of presentation.

[Participant 2] was also intrigued at modeling SIN and COS to determine angular speed constants. He said: "I tend to do it by trial and error. On the plus side, doing this trial and error can help students get a feeling for how this variable relates to the period of the function."

[Participant 3] offered a technical hint on utilizing the computer as an electronic chalkboard: "I connect my computer to a 27-inch TV monitor."

Conjectures and misconceptions, uncertainty and believing data, trial and error vs. modeling, and novel presentation. Hmmmm...

Which values or drawbacks added with this technology seem the most relevant to you?

Can you expand a bit on where and why you see value? Or challenges?

[Moderator]

The moderator links all of the questions by asking participants to consider the central assignment: What value does the software add?

TWO POLES OF INTERACTION

The control seeking behind *hijacking the dialogue* and the inattention and somnambulance of *whoosh, it went right by* are two poles of interaction within a dialogue. Clearly, to be an effective moderator, you must steer a middle course between these poles.

The eight types of roadblocks we've identified in this chapter are generalizations and are certainly not an exhaustive list. However, we've observed these forms many times in the hundreds of moderator postings in Concord Consortium netcourses.

As we noted in earlier chapters, the craft of moderating as a "Guide on the Side" shares many characteristics with counseling. We offer these general patterns of roadblocks for your consideration and use as you move away from center stage and try out methods of interaction that resemble guiding or counseling rather than direct instruction. These patterns will give you a simple, instructive framework that will allow you to analyze your own postings and help others develop postings that recognize and avoid ineffective or self-defeating styles.

In the netcourse offered to readers interested in practicing the methodology described in this book, we recently had a student comment on the roadblocks you've just read about. Perhaps you'll enjoy his comment as much as we do. He wrote:

> The authors provide an authoritative guide to moderating, but
> with little recrafting their text could become the transcript of a

"Sages Anonymous" meeting — "Hello, my name is _____ and I'm a recovering Sage-on-the-Stage. Those of you who've been here in the past have heard me talk about being a question mill or standing in the middle, commenting after each student's contribution, or about creating incoherence by losing sight of which details really matter. In this meeting I want to talk about another way that I hijack classes — I'm 'just a good student' along with my students. Just today, ..."

It helps to know I'm not the only one.

With careful coaching — perhaps aided by dialogue with a working group of facilitators who are seeking constructive input on their own online moderating efforts — you can indeed learn to become an effective online moderator. We wish you well in your quest, and we hope the signposts we've identified in this book will serve you as well as they've served us. Good luck!

Epilogue

EVALUATION
OF SUCCESS

▶

Facilitating Online Learning has offered a theoretical framework and a practical guide to help you meet the challenges of starting and sustaining quality dialogue in online courses or working groups. The system of voices and critical-thinking strategies we've outlined here provides an effective and adaptable set of pathways for both analysis of dialogues and composition of interventions so that you can leverage more-focused or deepened attention toward the objectives of any virtual community.

Maybe you're excited by these ideas; or maybe you're interested in them but you want to reserve judgment until you've tried the techniques for yourself. In any case, before attempting these methods that support a "Guide on the Side" educational approach, you need to explore a key issue: How will you know if you're facilitating in this "Guide on the Side" manner well or poorly?

One indication that you are indeed functioning well as a "Guide on the Side" may be an uneasiness or a sense of your own placelessness in the community you're leading. While noting considerable assistance from a moderator training workshop and an online moderator discussion group, one moderator we worked with frequently wrote about an uncomfortable level of frustration in attempting to model the "Guide on the Side" approach:

> I know that I want to interact with students/participants in a (Guide on the Side) manner, but I'm having trouble figuring out how to do it. Am I one of the participants, or am I outside the group itself?

Other moderators have felt discouraged:

> I felt that I was invisible — that my carefully crafted postings
> were being ignored by the participants.

Some moderators have felt quite awkward in writing with a style that relies very heavily on quoting others' contributions and not adding their own ideas. Said one:

> It feels a bit like plagiarism. I'm citing others' words so often in
> my writing.

Other moderators have found the idea of writing with another voice intriguing, but quite challenging when it comes time to compose interventions. Said one:

> I wasn't sure who I was when doing this writing.

Another stated:

> I had not realized how much I depended on visual feedback
> when in a classroom or a tutorial situation.

A common thread in all of these comments: When you the moderator interact as a "Guide on the Side" and employ the voices and critical-thinking framework we've outlined in this book, you'll likely feel a very different sense of authorship, as well as a different sense of personal feedback from your participants.

Placing her finger on a key issue — emotional satisfaction — one past moderator remarked:

> I realize now that it is harder to get a similar emotional satis-
> faction from the online situation [as opposed to a face-to-face
> interaction].

If you expect or need a continuous round of personal gratification, a "Guide on the Side" approach will likely prove disappointing for you. A "Guide on the Side" is not in the middle of things, stirring things up, or entertaining with his or her wit, style, or technical prowess. The work you accomplish as a "Guide on the Side" facilitator is evident in the adaptation of *participants'* ideas and in new ways of mirroring *participants'* thoughts.

"Partly invisible" accurately describes your interactions as a facilitator. This invisibility can prove to be a serious source of frustration and annoyance.

But you must consider what it is that grounds your need to be visible in a group. Several weeks after making the "feeling invisible" comment in the moderator's discussion area, the moderator mentioned above returned to share insights she'd gleaned from viewing dozens of recent postings. Ideas she'd highlighted and juxtaposed, and metaphors and tensions she'd helped clarify, were visible throughout the dialogue area. She had not seen the impact of her work initially. But later, her emotional satisfaction was great — though it was not the result of public praise. The group members had gone forward to discover the scope of their *own* ideas — thanks to the groundwork and vision laid (mostly anonymously) by the moderator's interventions.

It's only natural to feel uncomfortable when conventional methods, such as relying on your own carefully conceived positions or your personal voice, aren't available to help you articulate and represent ideas. But effective online moderation demands flexibility and a capacity to change your voice and style to reflect the needs of others.

A second indicator of effective "Guide on the Side" moderation is more direct. Though not a subject of study, the repertoire of styles of interaction and response supported by the voices and the critical-thinking strategies described in this book should start appearing in participants' interchanges — as a result of your continued usage. If this is happening, participants will commonly begin their postings by citing others' notes in shortened form; they'll then start posing and responding to questions that are set crisply by the critical-thinking frameworks.

In other words, your efforts to capture discussions through metaphors, intriguing comparisons, or shifts in the levels of conversation will be taken up by the participants themselves. Participants begin recognizing the need to sharpen a discussion's focus or think more deeply about certain matters, and their new insights begin to appear as central to their postings. If you've done a good job of laying the support framework for pragmatic dialogue, the participants begin, at least partially, to facilitate their own dialogue. Participant responses commonly become shorter and more targeted to central topics. Social and argumentative forms of dialogue take up a smaller fraction of the exchanges. Participants openly explore the rationale for their positions, or open for examination the assumptions they now see as underscoring some of their thinking.

In short, the participants internalize your internal monologue as commentator, clarifier, and questioner of thoughts.

Where can the "Guide on the Side" voice and critical-thinking strategy framework ultimately take your working group or netcourse? We don't know, and we cannot hazard a guess. Application of new ideas brings evolutionary changes to all shareholders in a dialogue. Change means growth. Changes in methods of dialogue are often accompanied by tension, periods of instability, or even regression. But there are always parallel movements toward greater clarity and focus and increased complexity.

Our framework of voices and critical-thinking strategies isn't intended as a final and complete list of the modes of interaction and composition for your online group. But it is, we believe, an effective guide that will help you and other facilitators develop new capacities leading to greater depth of online dialogue — and, of course, enhanced learning among the participants you lead.

GLOSSARY

Active Engagement. In a learning context, students are "actively engaged" when they are interacting with the material being taught. In an online environment, such engagement emerges, and can be seen, in student posts to discussions or assignment areas of the course.

Asynchronous Interactions. Online courses permit interactions across the barriers of time and distance. Asynchronous interactions, as contrasted with chat or audio- or video-conferencing environments, are generally in written form and are read by participants at times suitable to them. Often a record of past asynchronous dialogue is available for view from an archive. Ideas from postings that are days, weeks, or even months old can rekindle new dialogue if they are seen as relevant by participants or the moderator.

Authoritarian Communication. The authoritarian voice seeks to control and direct interactions by means of perceived or created rank or status. The purpose, however disguised by elegant or even persuasive content, is to influence and even control the flow and content of a dialogue.

Authoritative Communication. An authoritative voice or presence is quite necessary at many points in a dialogue. An authoritative voice speaks with the weight of scholarship, refined and sophisticated thinking, and personal and perhaps collective testimony to factual or perhaps theoretical stands on a topic. The product of an authoritative entry to a dialogue is the contribution of knowledge from accepted sources. It is possible for a contribution to be both authoritarian (see "Authoritarian Communication" above) and authoritative if it attempts to influence and control by appealing to personal stature or weight of opinions of others cited.

Bandwidth. Technically, bandwidth refers to the rate at which a computer is served by its connection to the Internet. High-bandwidth connections, like T-1 lines or cable modems, make it easy to download audio or video files. Low-bandwidth connections, on the other hand, are suitable only for text and limited multimedia usage.

Browser. Any computer software that permits a user to view and navigate World Wide Web sites at will. Some browsers may present text-only representations of the information received. Other browsers will display information with all of the multimedia elements it might contain.

Compressed File. To reduce transmission time when sharing files, systems or users often supply compressed versions of files, rather than full and perhaps lengthy files, for download. A compressed file can be many times smaller than the original. A decompression program is needed to expand the file back to its original format before it can be viewed.

"Conceptual Facilitator." One of six voices (see "Voice" below) a moderator or facilitator may assume in a dialogue intervention. As a Conceptual Facilitator, the moderator identifies conceptual areas that need attention. He or she then attempts to point out pieces of the conceptual landscape, so that participants can fill in or adjust any that are incomplete or don't quite make sense.

Constructivism. A theory of learning that assumes the deepest learning happens when students construct their own knowledge or seek their own meaning rather than learn by memorizing and practicing with rote drills and factual recall. Constructivism is oriented toward discovery, problem solving, and inquiry approaches to teaching, with the goal of fostering rich understanding.

Critical-Thinking Strategy. The logical form of any discussion intervention is determined by the critical-thinking strategy the moderator uses to compose it. Critical-thinking strategies come in two forms: those that sharpen the focus of the dialogue (see "Sharpening the Focus" below), and those that dig deeper into the dialogue (see "Deepening the Dialogue" below).

Deepening the Dialogue. To push dialogue forward so that participants explore ideas more richly, a moderator must make a decision: Does the dialogue need a bit more focusing on what directions may be fruitful or which terms need crisper meanings? If the moderator concludes that the common ground is covered well enough, he or she can seek to facilitate discussion beyond familiar applications and connections, so that participants explore new meanings and deepen their understandings. This process is known as deepening the dialogue.

Dialogue Elements. Any element of a contribution by a participant or the moderator is termed a dialogue element. Dialogue elements may include quotes by participants or citations of experts, images, audio or video files, site references, or assignments.

Discussion Area. Most online courseware for the World Wide Web features a discussion area where participants can hold asynchronous, text-based discussions.

Emoticon. To help readers interpret text-based meaning in email and other online communications (e.g., chats, threaded discussions), a variety of symbols depicting facial expressions have become common. These emoticons must be "read" sideways (by tilting one's head to the left), as in the case of this smiley face: :-) A number of common emoticons are listed in Chapter 4.

Facilitator. We've used the terms facilitator and moderator interchangeably throughout this book, but their meanings differ slightly. Moderating is part of a wider role of facilitating a course or online team task. As in any other context, a facilitator may be a leader or instructor, an outside observer serving a group, or simply a co-equal member who is taking a turn at facilitating. When doing this work online, one key role for the facilitator is to moderate the discussions, thus focusing and deepening the work of the group and enhancing outcomes or products of the communal effort.

FAQs (Frequently Asked Questions). Typical problems, along with their answers, are commonly collected and made available to participants as FAQ's, or Frequently Asked Questions. FAQs may focus on technical issues or on the general approach to dialogue or pedagogy online.

File Compression. See "Compressed File," above.

Flame/Flaming. To communicate emotionally and/or excessively via electronic means (e.g., email, chat, online dialogue). Flaming can take the form of online "cursing," "shouting," or name calling.

"Focusing on Key Points." One of six critical-thinking strategies (see "Critical-Thinking Strategy" above) identified and explained in this book. Using the focusing-on-key-points approach, the moderator works with participant input and draws on formal structures of the online experience, such as any specific goals for the group or conceptual organizers. The goal of the focusing-on-key-points intervention: to highlight essential concepts and connections made to date by the participants.

"Full-Spectrum Questioning." One of six critical thinking strategies (see "Critical-Thinking Strategy" above) identified and explained in this book. Full-spectrum questioning offers five general categories of questions, with each category designed to extract layers of meaning when applied to words, processes, statements, or directions of a dialogue. By modeling these richer modes of questioning, the moderator can help participants find new ways of viewing and questioning their own thinking.

"Generative Guide." One of six voices (see "Voice" below) a moderator or facilitator may assume in a dialogue intervention. In assuming the voice of a Generative Guide, the moderator lays out a spectrum of current or possible positions taken to indicate avenues of questioning that have remained overlooked or unexplored.

Graphics Interchange Format (.gif). .gif files are one of the common ways of coding and exchanging graphical information on the Internet.

"Guide on the Side." This term is commonly held up against the term "Sage on the Stage" (see "Sage on the Stage" below) to capture the difference between an expert lecturing to students who are expected to memorize information ("Sage on the Stage") and another kind of teacher who shares leadership with students and supports their work from the sidelines, more like a coach ("Guide on the Side").

"Hijacking the Dialogue." One of the common errors in online moderating in which the moderator, usually unknowingly, "takes over" the discussion.

Honoring Multiple Perspectives. One of six critical-thinking strategies (see "Critical-Thinking Strategy" above) identified and explained in this book. In general, the moderator uses the honoring-multiple-perspectives approach in mature dialogues, in which the participants are comfortable with detaching themselves from particular beliefs or assumptions and are amenable to considering widely differing viewpoints.

"Identifying Direction.**"** One of six critical-thinking strategies (see "Critical-Thinking Strategy" above) identified and explained in this book. By carefully reflecting upon the entries in a discussion thread, the moderator can assess the general tack of the dialogue, its progress, and what appear to be digressions from the goals for each activity or discussion topic.

Listserv. Software that relays emails that have been sent to a particular mailbox, set up by an administrator. The emails then go to the email addresses of all participants who have requested to receive them by "joining" or "subscribing to" the listserv. Listservs are commonly used to host Internet discussion groups.

Lotus Notes' "LearningSpace." One of many online courseware packages that can be used as a full educational "environment" on the World Wide Web.

Lurker. A participant may choose to limit his or her discussion interactions when a course begins. He or she commonly waits for others to comment on ideas or explore tensions. This practice is called lurking in a conversation, with the participant thus being referred to as a lurker.

"Making Connections." One of six critical-thinking strategies (see "Critical- Thinking Strategy" above) identified and explained in this book. A making-connections strategy challenges participants to go beyond "more of the same" to explore, at an individual and a group level, inferences, tensions, and perhaps rationales for statements in the discussion, and to move beyond first-look interpretations. Using the making connections strategy, the moderator attempts to help participants make shifts to deeper layers of meaning in their communications.

"Mediator." One of six voices (see "Voice" below) a moderator or facilitator may assume in a dialogue intervention. In support of the central goal — maintaining the dialogue's direction and open spirit — a moderator using the voice of a Mediator redirects discussion away from defense of hardened positions and toward goals that are central to the interests of all parties..

Moderator. See "Facilitator," above.

Netcourse. A body of study offered via worldwide digital electronic communications. The term netcourse is derived from the term "network," which refers to a system of associated computers that allows users to share information.

'Netiquette. The online equivalent of the social skills and understandings covered by the term etiquette in face-to-face environments. Participants and moderators must pay attention to possible perceptions of their entries in online communication. Since these entries are typically in written form, they can easily, albeit unintentionally, offend or insult others, or, less harmfully, appear as insensitive or boorish.

Participant. A student in an online course.

Password. When signing onto a course, or even some listserv dialogues, users are given a username (see "Username" below) and a password. Together, the proper username and password permit the user access to private Internet spaces. They also ensure that the person visiting is really the owner of the access account — unless, of course, one or both have been stolen by someone else.

"Personal Muse." One of six voices (see "Voice" below) a moderator or facilitator may assume in a dialogue intervention. The Personal Muse approach models, in a public forum, the kind of internal dialogue anyone might have with himself or herself when critically examining his or her beliefs.

Post. To send an electronic communication, generally to a threaded (see "Thread/Threaded Discussion" below) discussion group or a listserv (see "Listserv" above) that is supporting dialogue on a topic. The term can also refer to sending an email to an instructor or another student. In noun form, a post (or posting) refers to that which a moderator or participant "posts" for discussion.

"Reflective Guide." One of six voices (see "Voice" below) a moderator or facilitator may assume in a dialogue intervention. The Reflective Guide restates or recrafts, with slightly different emphasis, the elements of a message or sequence of messages. A Reflective Guide posting carries a sense of non-directive interaction, as effected by a Rogerian counselor, though the dialogue itself is goal-directed.

Rich-Text Format (.rtf). .rtf is a data protocol for exchanging files between word processors. Exchange of text is rather easily accomplished. Files containing graphics or complex formatting, however, can cause problems if both users are not using the same version of the same word processor. Saving and exchanging files as .rtf documents usually resolves compatibility/readability issues. Note, however, that an .rtf file can be many times greater in size than the original.

"Role Play" (Character Identification). One of six voices (see "Voice" below) a moderator or facilitator may assume in a dialogue intervention. In using a Role Player (or Character Identification) strategy, a moderator can introduce necessary alternative perspectives into a dialogue without concern for personal ownership or direct confrontation of participants.

"Sage on the Stage." This term is commonly held up against the term "Guide on the Side" (see "Guide on the Side" above) to capture the difference between an expert lecturing to students who are expected to memorize information ("Sage on the Stage") and another kind of teacher who shares leadership with students and supports their work from the sidelines, more like a coach ("Guide on the Side").

Screen Shot. There are built-in options in both PC and Mac systems, as well as several shareware programs, that allow users to take a "snapshot" of whatever is on their computer screens. Such a snapshot, saved as an image file, is referred to as a screen shot.

Sharpening the Focus. Using a sharpening-the-focus strategy, a moderator focuses and constrains discussions by making careful sense of ideas and clarifying them to create common ground. Ideas and directions are sorted out, and consensus on the direction of the dialogue is negotiated. Sharpening the focus is the first challenge a moderator faces in a new dialogue. He or she must strive to build and maintain clarity and direction before directing the group into deeper waters.

Social Dialogue. Social dialogue is a critical aspect of healthy communication, usually prominent at the beginning or end of a meeting or a statement by a new contributor to a discussion. The purpose of social dialogue is related more to building community than to the content participants might ultimately delve into. Thus, the content of social dialogue varies widely, from jokes to weather to personal news to how people are feeling.

Software Version Civility. One can never assume that the files created by his or her word processor, or the formats he or she is using for images, are readable by others. Software version civility refers to participants paying attention to such details when they attempt to share documents with each other.

"Sorting Ideas for Relevance." One of six critical-thinking strategies (see "Critical-Thinking-Strategy" above) identified and explained in this book. In a sorting-for-relevance post, the moderator identifies candidates for primary issues. He or she then identifies the issues that might be tangents or digressions, and that, however appealing, the group should leave for another time.

Synchronous Interactions. Communications in real time, such as those via the telephone, videophones, or live text chats. Online game playing can also be synchronous.

Text-Only File (.txt). .txt files contain only ASCII characters. They are commonly opened in the "NotePad" utility on PCs and in the "Simpletext" program on Macintoshes.

Thread/Threaded Discussion. Threaded discussion refers to an asynchronous method of communicating in which comments to an original post are listed below, and indented under, the original post. Comments to comments are indented again. A thread refers to the full list of comments, including the original post and all the comments participants made to it. A discussion may feature multiple threads.

Tone. Any communication, oral or written, employs a tone. In text-based communication, tone can be more easily misinterpreted because facial and audio cues aren't supporting the bare words (as is the case in most face-to-face communications). Adding tone, purposefully, to text-based communication by using emoticons (see "Emoticons" above) or such words as "ha ha!" helps address the potential for misinterpretations.

Unthreaded Discussion. Email is the most common unthreaded discussion mechanism. It's possible for a system to display a series of emails on a topic, usually sorted by message subject. A series of comments then appears as a simple list.

Username. When signing onto a course, or even some listserv dialogues, users are given a username and a password (see "Password" above). Together, the proper username and password permit the user access to private Internet spaces. They also ensure that the person visiting is really the owner of the access account — unless, of course, one or both have been stolen by someone else.

Virtual "Hand Holding." This term describes what many people seem to need when they first get online or when they first start using a new kind of online technology. The essential ingredient for progress is a kind, helpful voice on the other end that guides them personally through the basic steps, even if clear instructions are already available to them. This guiding is referred to as virtual "hand holding."

"Voice." Any communication, oral or written, employs a voice. We use the term in a limited, technical sense in this book. The moderator enters into discussions using one of many voices, which are also referred to as personas, characters, or masks. The goal of the moderator's communication is not the expression of a personal or creative vision; rather, it is to clarify and extend the thinking of other people. To this end, the moderator selects a voice, which may or may not feel comfortable, to help the participants see their own thinking for a specific time or context in the dialogue. Thus, the voice in this context is really a tool that facilitates others' reflections and pre-presentations of their ideas, with the purpose of moving the dialogue or learning forward.

Wait Time. The number of seconds an instructor waits before calling on another student or responding to a question or comment. In the face-to-face environment, wait time has been shown to increase significantly both the amount and quality of reactions by students.

"Wallowing in the Shallows." A common state of affairs in online and face-to-face courses. Participants remain outside the main ideas and don't directly engage them. Nor do they confront and explore their own assumptions about what is being said or what is really central and what is not.

"Whoosh, It Went Right By." Though seemingly a fanciful and inept coinage, this term accurately describes a common problem in online courses. The moderator's attention can be directed toward specific outcomes; thus, the moderator may fail to observe and highlight for others elegant and insightful pieces of dialogue that can potentially add much richness and context to the discussion.

REFERENCES

■ ■ ■ ■ ■ ■ ■ ■ ■ ■

Argyris, Chris. 1982. *Reasoning, learning, and action: Individual and organizational.* San Francisco: Jossey-Bass, Publishers.

Argyris, Chris. 1985. *Strategy, change, and defensive routines.* Boston: Pitman.

Argyris, Chris, and Donald Schon. 1992. *Theory in practice: Increasing professional effectiveness.* San Francisco: Jossey-Bass, Publishers.

Bohm, David. 1990. *On dialogue.* Ojai, CA: David Bohm Seminars.

Dewey, John. 1938. *Logic: The theory of inquiry.* New York: Holt.

Drucker, Peter. 1988. *The age of discontinuity: Guidelines to our changing society.* New York: Warner Books.

Hartmann, William K., and Joe Cain. 1995. *Craters! A multi-science approach to cratering and impacts.* Arlington, VA: National Science Teachers Association.

Lippman, Matthew. 1991. *Thinking in education.* New York: Cambridge University Press.

Matthies, Dennis. 1996. *Precision questioning.* Palo Alto, CA: Center for Teaching and Learning, Stanford University.

National Research Council. 1991. *National science education standards.* Washington, DC: National Academy Press.

Paul, Richard. 1990. *Critical thinking.* Rohnert Park, CA: Center for Critical Thinking and Moral Critique.

Peters, Tom, and Robert H. Waterman H. 1988. *In search of excellence: Lessons from America's best-run companies.* New York: Warner Books.

Rorty, Richard. 1979. *Philosophy and the mirror of nature.* Princeton, NJ: Princeton University Press.

References
■■■■■■■■■■

Schon, Donald. 1983. *The reflective practitioner: How professionals think in action.* New York: Basic Books.

Senge, Peter M. 1990. *The fifth discipline: The art and practice of the learning organization.* New York: Doubleday.

Shah, Idries. 1971 *Thinkers of the east: Studies in experimentalism.* London, Octagon Press.